The Amazing Laws of Cosmic Mind Power

Joseph Murphy, Ph.D., D.D.

Revised by Ian D. McMahan

REWARD BOOKS

REWARD BOOKS
An imprint of Prentice Hall Press
A member of Penguin Putnam Inc.
375 Hudson Street
New York, New York 10014
www.penguinputnam.com

Library of Congress Cataloging-in-Publication Data

Murphy, Joseph
   The amazing laws of cosmic mind power / Joseph Murphy ; revised by
Ian D. McMahan
      p. cm.
   ISBN 0-7352-0220-6
   1. New Thought.   I. McMahan, Ian.   II. Title.

BF639.M815   2001
299'.93—dc21   2001019054

Printed in the United States of America

10   9   8   7   6   5   4   3   2

Most Reward Books are available at special quantity discounts for bulk purchases for
sales promotions, premiums, fund-raising, or educational use. Special books, or book
excerpts, can also be created to fit specific needs.

For details, write: Special Markets, Penguin Putnam Inc., 375 Hudson Street, New
York, New York 10014.

CONTENTS

PREFACE *ix*

LAW 1 The Astounding Law of Contact
with the Cosmic Mind   1

THE MIRACLE OF PRAYER **2**   PRAYER CAN CHANGE YOUR LIFE
4   YOU CAN BECOME WHAT YOU LONG TO BE **5**   A PRAYER
FOR FORGIVENESS **6**   HOW INFINITE INTELLIGENCE ANSWERED
HIS PRAYER **8**   PRAYER OVERCOMES RACIAL PREJUDICE **9**
PRAYER OPENS PRISON DOORS **10**   HER PRAYER SAVED HIM
FROM FINANCIAL DISASTER **12**   YOUR DAILY PRAYER **14**
POINTS TO REMEMBER **15**

LAW 2   The Secret Law of Faith   17

FAITH-POWER WORKS WONDERS **18**   EVERYONE HAS FAITH
20   FAITH IN THE INVISIBLE **20**   HOW HIS FAITH TRIUMPHED
21   SHE CHANGED HER FAITH **24**   HIS FAITH MADE HIM
WHOLE **25**   FAITH IS YOUR MIND **27**   HER FAITH IN
INFINITE INTELLIGENCE **28**   SERVE YOURSELF WITH
FAITH-POWER **30**

LAW 3   The Miraculous Law of Healing   32

HEALED OF SPIRIT-VOICES **33**   SHE WASN'T EXPECTED TO LIVE
35   THE NATURAL-BORN HEALER **37**   DEGREES OF FAITH **38**
A CASE OF PALSY **38**   SHE HEALED HER WITHERED HAND **40**
HOW THE HOPELESS CASE WAS HEALED **42**   BLIND FAITH AND
TRUE FAITH **44**   HOW TO GIVE A SPIRITUAL TREATMENT **45**
VERY PROFITABLE POINTERS **46**   HOW YOU CAN FACE THE

WORD *INCURABLE* IN YOUR OWN LIFE *47* HEALING OF DROPSY *48* STEPS IN HEALING *50* SPIRITUAL BLINDNESS *51* VISION IS SPIRITUAL, ETERNAL, AND INDESTRUCTIBLE *52* SPECIAL PRAYER FOR EYES AND EARS *52* STEP THIS WAY FOR A HEALING *53*

LAW 4   The Dynamic Law of Protection   55

A NEW CONCEPT OF GOD WORKS WONDERS *57* WHY SHE HAD NO BOYFRIENDS *58* HOW HE BECAME A SUPERIOR STUDENT *60* HE COULD NOT BE SHOT *61* YOUR ANSWER DETERMINES YOUR FUTURE *62* YOUR BELIEF ABOUT GOD IS YOUR BELIEF ABOUT YOURSELF *63* BELIEVE IN A GOD OF LOVE *64* BECOMING A NEW PERSON *64* HIS BUSINESS PROSPERED THREE-HUNDRED PERCENT *65* THE MIRACLE OF THREE STEPS *66* THE COUPLE WAS REUNITED *68* THE TRANSFORMING POWER OF LOVE *69* PRAYER TRANSFORMED A CRIMINAL *71* PRAYER SAVED HIS LIFE *72* THE POWER OF GOD *73* POINTS TO REMEMBER *74*

LAW 5 The Mysterious Law of Inner Guidance   77

FOLLOW THE LEAD THAT COMES *78* THERE ALWAYS IS AN ANSWER *78* A BUSINESSWOMAN'S GUIDANCE FORMULA *79* A PROFESSOR GETS A SPECIFIC ANSWER *81* ALWAYS BE ON THE ALERT *83* BE STILL AND RELAXED *83* SHE GETS WONDERFUL SLOGANS *84* INTUITION PAYS FABULOUS DIVIDENDS *84* HOW A NOVELIST GETS MARVELOUS IDEAS *85* HE FOUND HIS TRUE PLACE *85* A PRAYER FOR DIVINE GUIDANCE *87* IDEAS TO REMEMBER *87*

LAW 6   The Mighty Law of Courage   90

HOW PRAYER FREED HER FROM PANIC *90*   HER PRAYER CAST OUT HER FEAR *92*   A GARDEN GAVE HIM COURAGE *93* HE CAST OUT HIS UNKNOWN FEARS *94*   SHE CEASED BLOCKING THE ANSWER *95*   WISE THOUGHTS *97*   CHOOSE CONFIDENCE, TRIUMPH, AND VICTORY *97*   HOW SHE OVERCAME THE FEELING OF FRUSTRATION *98*   FIVE POSITIONS IN FIVE MONTHS *100*   HOW TO REALIZE YOUR DESIRE *101* TAKE A PERSONAL INVENTORY *102* UNDERSTANDING BANISHES NEEDLESS SUFFERING *103*   YOU CREATE YOUR OWN HEAVEN *104*   RETRIBUTION AND REWARD *105*   THE SECRET PLACE *106*   IMPORTANT POINTERS *107*

LAW 7   The Wonderful Law of Security   109

HOW TO GET THE FEELING OF SECURITY *110*   HE STOPPED PRAYING AGAINST HIMSELF *111*   THE END OF MY ROPE *112* SECURITY CANNOT BE LEGISLATED *115*   PRAY AND PROTECT YOUR INVESTMENTS *115*   PRAYER CONTROLLED HIS UPS AND DOWNS *116*   HOW SHE HEALED HER SENSE OF LOSS *117*   BUILDING A GLORIOUS FUTURE *120*   A HEALTHY REVIEW *121*

LAW 8   The Magical Law of Mental Nutrition   123

YOU ARE WHAT YOU MENTALLY EAT *124*   THE IMPORTANCE OF DIET *124*   THE BREAD OF LOVE AND PEACE *125*   YOUR MENTAL AND SPIRITUAL DIET *126*   HER HEAD KNOWLEDGE BECAME HEART KNOWLEDGE *127*   HIS MENTAL IMAGERY HEALED HIM *129*   THE THANKFUL HEART *130*   HIGH-LIGHTS TO RECALL *131*

LAW 9   The Great Law of Love   133

LOVE IS ALWAYS OUTGOING *133*   HOW MUCH DO YOU WANT TO BE A NEW PERSON? *134*   WHY AN ACTOR FAILED THREE TIMES *134*   HIS PRAYER OF TRIUMPH *135*   LOVE OF GOD AND WHAT IT MEANS *136*   LOVE AND FEAR CANNOT DWELL TOGETHER *137*   LOVE CONQUERS JEALOUSY *138*   THE LORD GIVETH THE INCREASE *139*   HOW SHE PASSED HER EXAMINATION *141*   FEAR THOUGHTS CAN'T HURT YOU *142*   BECOME A SPIRITUAL GIANT *143*   LOST IN THE JUNGLE *143*   DON'T FIGHT FEAR *144*   THE ENEMY IN HER OWN MIND *145*   LOVE'S HEALING BALM *146*   BASIC POINTS TO REMEMBER *147*

LAW 10   The Positive Law of Emotional Control   149

BECOMING EMOTIONALLY MATURE *150*   GETTING THE RIGHT CONCEPT OF YOURSELF *150*   HOW SHE OVERCAME DEPRESSION *151*   HOW SHE OVERCAME BAD TEMPER *153*   HIS MENTAL PHOTOGRAPH *154*   YOU CAN CONTROL YOUR EMOTIONS *155*   THE EMOTION OF LOVE FREED HIM *156*   HOW YOUR EMOTIONS AFFECT YOUR BODY *156*   THE POSITIVE EMOTIONS OF FAITH AND CONFIDENCE *157*   WATCH YOUR REACTIONS *158*   YOU ARE LIVING IN TWO WORLDS *160*   HOW TO TRANSFORM YOURSELF *161*   PRAYER FOR CONTROLLING THE EMOTIONS *163* THINGS TO WATCH *163*

LAW 11   The Thrilling Law of Marital Harmony   166

LOVE UNITES AND FEAR DIVIDES *166*   THE TRUTH SET HIM FREE *168*   HE DEMANDED A DIVORCE *169*   MARRIED FIVE TIMES *171*   HOW HE FOUND HIS IDEAL *172*   THAT'S THE MAN I WANT *174*   LOVE IS A ONENESS *176*   AVOID A

DEAD-END STREET *176* SHOULD I GET A DIVORCE? *178*
GET A NEW ESTIMATE OF YOURSELF *179* BECOMING A
SUCCESSFUL HUSBAND OR WIFE *179* THE BIBLICAL FORMULA
180 MARRIAGE PRAYER FOR HUSBAND AND WIFE *181* STEP
THIS WAY TO A HAPPY MARRIAGE *182*

LAW 12   The Glorious Law
of Peace of Mind   184

HE WORRIED ABOUT WHAT HAD NOT HAPPENED *184* SHE
HEALED HER ANXIETY NEUROSIS *187* HIS WORRY WAS NOT
CAUSED BY HIS PROBLEM *189* HOW SHE GOT OFF THE
MERRY-GO-ROUND *192* YOU DON'T WANT IT *193*
HOW WORRY AFFECTS ALL GLANDS AND ORGANS OF OUR
BODIES *193* HE RAISED HIS SIGHTS *194* YOU CAN
OVERCOME WORRY *195* STEPS IN PRAYER FOR OVERCOMING
WORRY *196* POWER-POINTERS *197*

LAW 13   The Replenishing Law
of Automatic Prosperity   199

HOW A BROKER PROSPERED *200* HIS SUBCONSCIOUS PAID
HIS MORTGAGE *201* THE MAGIC OF INCREASE *203*
"THANK YOU" OPENS THE WAY TO PROSPERITY *204* LIFE IS
ADDITION *206* SHE BEGAN TO SELL AGAIN *206* HIS
SUBCONSCIOUS MADE HIM A MILLIONAIRE *207* PRAYER FOR
PROSPERITY *209* SOME PROFITABLE POINTERS *210*

LAW 14   The Penultimate Law
of Creation   212

HOW HE BECAME PRESIDENT *213* HER CREATIVE
IMAGINATION HEALED HER *214* HER IMAGINATION HEALED
HERSELF AND HER FAMILY *216* IMAGINING PRODUCES A

GREAT TEACHER _217_ SCIENCE AND IMAGINATION _218_
GREAT ACCOMPLISHMENTS THROUGH IMAGINING _218_
IMAGINING BROUGHT HER SUCCESS AND RECOGNITION _219_
IMAGINING PROMOTED A CHEMIST _220_ HOW IMAGINATION
MAKES THE PAST ALIVE _221_ GRADUATES WITH HONORS
THROUGH IMAGINING _221_ A BOY HEALED HIS MOTHER
THROUGH IMAGING _223_ IMAGINATION, THE WORKSHOP OF
GOD _224_ USING YOUR IMAGINATION _225_

LAW 15   The Ultimate Law
of Infinite Life   228

HOW TO BEGIN _229_ HE FOUND HIS SON AFTER SEVEN
YEARS _229_ HER HOME WAS SAVED _230_ SHE
ACKNOWLEDGED THE PRESENCE _231_ HIS AUDIENCE LOVES
HIM NOW _232_ HOW BROTHER LAWRENCE PRACTICED THE
PRESENCE _234_ SHE HEALED HER SON _235_ HE WALKED
AND TALKED _236_ HE COULD NOT BE RUINED _237_
PRACTICE THE THREE STEPS _238_ DWELLING WITH GOD _239_
RECALLING GREAT TRUTHS _240_

Index   243

PREFACE

This book can work what may seem like magic in your life.

Magic is the production of effects by forces we do not yet understand. As you grow to appreciate the processes, they cease to seem magical, but they remain marvelous. Suppose someone from a distant century watched you using the Internet to retrieve information from a database half a world away, then exchange instant messages with a friend in another state, all the while listening to a symphony played by a full orchestra on a compact disc. Your visitor would be convinced that you were a world-class magician or sorcerer. It is because we have some notion of how these devices work that they do not seem magical to us.

All fundamental forces are, by their nature, unknown. Furthermore, all things are the products of mind, yet we do not really know what mind is. We cannot analyze it under a microscope, nor can we see it, but we can find out, nevertheless, how it works. Then we discover a hidden power that lifts us up and sets us on the high road to happiness, freedom, and peace of mind.

How You Use Your Cosmic Power Every Day

We don't know what electricity is. We know some of the things it does, but the inner nature of this force is still unknown to us. So, you see, all of us actually use special powers all day long. We don't understand, for example, how we move or can lift a finger just by the express will of the mind. It is said that the lifting of a finger disturbs the most distant star. So you see that we all are familiar enough with what might be called magic, even though it does not go by that name in our common speech. It is only the unaccustomed thing we do not understand that we call magic.

You have a mind and you will learn how to use it more effectively in the pages of this book. As a result, wonders will happen in your life.

How This Book Can Change Your Life

This book contains the key to rebuilding your entire life. It is written for you. In the fifteen chapters of this book, in simple, practical, down-to-earth language, techniques and processes are set forth for using the magical powers of the Universal Mind within you to bring forth health, happiness, and prosperity, plus a feeling of complete inner satisfaction and fulfillment.

As you read the captivating and enthralling stories in these pages, you will see exactly how others have accomplished startling things through the special powers within them. This book shows you how to change yourself from within. The Cosmic Power is within you. The information on these pages shows you how to find it and how to use it.

Why None of Your Problems Need to Go Unsolved

There is an answer to every problem. I definitely believe you will find your answer in the pages of this book. Universal Mind Power is the greatest power in the world. Whatever you desire, this Power can fulfill that desire for you. The Power is your mind, which is one with the Universal Mind.

This book describes how to think and what to think and how to direct your mind so that miracles will happen in your life. You will find priceless knowledge in these pages that makes it possible for you to banish forever the deadly mental poisons of fear, worry, and jealousy.

As you read and then apply the special power of your mind as outlined herein, you will set out on a great and wonderful adventure in mental and spiritual unfoldment. This journey will pay you fabulous dividends in health, wealth, love, and expression. It will prove very exciting, and thereafter you will look forward to the future with joy and enthusiasm. Continue in your marvelous journey through this book until the day breaks and all the shadows flee.

LAW 1

THE ASTOUNDING LAW OF CONTACT WITH THE COSMIC MIND

Prayer is always the solution. God is . . . *a very present help in [time of] trouble* (Ps. 46:1). We are told that we should *pray, believing* (Matt. 21:22), and we shall receive. If this is so—and daily proofs surround us—then prayer is the greatest force in all the world.

No matter what the problem might be, no matter how great the difficulty or how complicated the matter seems to be, prayer can solve it and bring about a happy and joyous solution. After having prayed, you take whatever practical steps seem indicated, because your prayer will guide and direct your footsteps.

Prayer is contacting, communicating with, and aligning your thought with the Infinite Intelligence, which responds to the nature of your thought and belief. Prayer will bring forth whatever you want and need in your life, if you conform to the laws of your mind purposefully, sincerely, and righteously. Prayer constantly brings about the seemingly impossible and heals the so-called incurable. In the history of humankind, there is no conceivable problem that has not at some time been solved by prayer.

People of all ages, all countries, and all religions have believed in the miraculous power of prayer. *God is no respecter of persons* (Acts 10:34) and He is available to all people, regardless of their race, creed, or color. Those who have received marvelous answers to their prayers have either consciously or unconsciously given recognition, honor, and devotion to a responsive Infinite Intelligence that indwells all humans.

Remember that God is omnipotent, omniscient, and omnipresent, and is untrammeled by time, space, matter, or the vagaries of humankind. It is easy to see, therefore, that there can be no limit to the power of prayer, because *with God all things are possible* (Matt. 19:26).

THE MIRACLE OF PRAYER

More than sixty years ago, a man was convicted of murder in one of our western states. He was sentenced to be hanged. During the time between his trial and the date set for his execution, he discovered the love of God. He prayed that God would forgive him and spare him. The man had committed the murder for which he had been sentenced, but he had heard or read that God was "the bad man's deliverer." He took this thought to heart and pondered it every day. When the day came and he was led to the gallows, the trap, which ordinarily would fall the moment it was released, jammed in place. The hangman and his assistants tried again and again to spring the trap, but it was of no use. Finally, the prisoner was led back to his cell. Eventually he was granted a reprieve. In later years he became a spiritual inspiration to his fellow prisoners.

The love of God indeed passes all understanding and illuminates the path we tread. The wonders and blessings of God know no end.

God does not condemn or judge any person. The Bible says: *Thou art of purer eyes than to behold evil, and canst not look on iniquity . . .* (Hab. 1:13). You pass judgment on yourself by the concepts and beliefs that you entertain. You are always choosing thoughts, and in that act you are passing judgment on yourself. God, however, sees you as perfect. The Perfect One cannot see imperfection. When you rise in consciousness to the point that you forgive yourself and cleanse your mind and heart, the past is forgotten. It becomes as if it never were.

So often, we are told that "As you sow, so shall you reap." This is an oversimplification. Yes, reaping what you have sown is a law of the world, but only so long as you do not pray or meditate on the truths of God. No matter how awful the crime or how heinous the offense, it can be wiped away from the mind, together with all the punishment that would ordinarily follow. Mere affirmations and perfunctory prayer will not change matters, however. What is essential is a deep hunger and thirst for God's love and peace, plus an intense desire to reform. It is this combination that has the power to wipe away the punishment that must otherwise follow destructive thinking.

PRAYER CAN CHANGE YOUR LIFE

About twenty years ago, in England, I had a long talk with a man who confessed to me that he had once killed a man. The circumstances were not all black—he had thought he was defending himself—but there it was. He intensely wanted to transform himself, to be reborn mentally and spiritually. At the end of our interview, I wrote a special prayer for him. I suggested that he spend fifteen or twenty minutes, several times daily, meditating on it. He was quietly, silently, and lovingly to claim and feel that God's love, peace, beauty, glory, and joy were flowing through his mind and heart, purifying, cleansing, healing, and restoring his soul. As he did this regularly, these attributes of God were gradually resurrected within him.

A few months later, he told me that one night his whole mind and body, as well as the room he was in, became a blaze of light. Like Paul, he was actually blinded for a while by the light. He told me that all he could remember was that he knew the whole world was within him and that he felt the ecstasy and rapture of God's love. His feeling was indescribable. It was the moment that lasts forever. Truly, he was a changed man; he experienced and expressed divine love in his mind and heart. I learned that eventually he began to teach others how to live, and I am sure that he is still doing it somewhere.

YOU CAN BECOME
WHAT YOU LONG TO BE

Arthur T. came to me for counseling. "I can't seem to hold down a job," he said. "I suppose some people might say it's my own fault. I can't really throw myself into my work. In fact, sometimes I can't even be bothered to show up. It's all so worldly and irrelevant. I have my mind set on higher things."

"What do you mean?" I asked.

"There's only one thing that matters," he replied. "And that is going to heaven when I die. Everything else is trivial, right?"

"Not exactly," I said. "What we call heaven is really another term for the mind at peace. In the framework of cosmic consciousness, there is no such thing as physical death. The only real death is a psychological process, in which you allow your spiritual faculties to be smothered by ignorance, fear, superstition, and sloth. And from what you say, you are in real danger of dying that death."

His face took on a frightened look. "Tell me, what can I do?" he begged.

"You must work to resurrect faith, zeal, enthusiasm, confidence, and true expression in your life," I replied.

At my suggestion, Arthur began to pray that Infinite Intelligence would guide and direct him to true expression and that he would prosper spiritually, mentally, and financially. Gradually, he began to develop a new interest and excitement in life and to apply himself vigorously to his work. Soon he not only held his job but was promoted to a more responsible position. His new mental attitude changed everything in his life. He described these wonderful changes to me, then added, "I don't have to brood over my chances of going to heaven. I am living in heaven now."

A PRAYER FOR FORGIVENESS

Doreen B. told me that she had never recovered from the abuse she suffered as a child. She was raised by an aunt and uncle after her parents were killed in an accident.

"It still haunts me," she said. "I wake up every day asking myself how anyone could torment a little kid that way. No matter how hard I tried, I was punished for making a mess, for making noise, for not doing my chores fast enough or well enough. It was awful!"

"Why do you think they treated you that way?" I asked.

"It was part of their beliefs," she said. "They thought they were driving the devil out of me. And everything I did was just one more sign that they hadn't done it yet."

Her eyes filled with tears.

"And do you know what's really terrible?" she continued after a moment. "They convinced me. Whenever anything goes wrong for me, right away I think, 'I must have deserved this.' Hard as I try, I can't forgive myself for not being perfect."

I explained to Doreen that forgiving herself meant extending that same forgiveness to those who had harmed her. "Remember the words of the Bible: *And when ye stand praying, forgive, if ye have ought against any . . .* (Mark 11:25)."

I then taught her a simple but effective method to bring about forgiveness in herself. "Think of God and His love for you," I told her. "Quiet your mind, relax, and let go. Then affirm this prayer."

> I fully and freely forgive [think of the name of the offender]. I release him or her mentally and spiritually. I completely forgive everything connected with the matter in question. I am free, and he or she is free. It is a marvelous feeling.
>
> This is my day of general amnesty. I release anybody and everybody who has ever hurt me, and I wish for each and everyone health, happiness, peace, and all the blessings of life. I do this freely, joyously, and lovingly. Whenever I think of the person or persons who hurt me, I say, "I have released you, and all the blessings of life are yours." I am free and they are free. It is wonderful!

As Doreen discovered, the great secret of true forgiveness is that once you have forgiven a person, it is unnecessary to repeat the prayer. Whenever the person comes to your mind or the particular hurt happens to enter your mind, wish the person well, and say, "Peace be unto you." Do this as often as the thought enters your mind. After a few days, thoughts of the person or experience will return less and less often, until they fade into nothingness.

HOW INFINITE INTELLIGENCE ANSWERED HIS PRAYER

Many years ago I lectured in Auckland, New Zealand at the Temple of Higher Thought. Douglas R. spoke to me at the end of one of my lectures. "Two years ago, my daughter moved to America, to New York City," he said. "We have not been able to see each other since. I desperately want to go visit her, but I can't afford it."

"Did you hear today's lecture?" I asked

"Yes, of course," he replied. "But . . ."

"I understand your doubts," I said. "But you must teach yourself to set them aside. Try this: Several times a day, go to a quiet place, relax, and affirm, *Infinite Intelligence opens up the way for me to visit my daughter in New York City in divine order.* Every evening, before going to sleep, visualize yourself in the airport terminal in New York. Make the picture as clear and realistic as you can. Your daughter is giving you a big welcome hug and saying, 'Daddy, I am so glad to see you at last.' See the joy on her face and hear the love in her voice."

"I'll try it," he promised.

Before I left Auckland, I received a phone call at my hotel. It was Douglas. "A miracle has happened," he announced. "Years ago I was in business with a partner who cheated me out of several thousand pounds. Today I received a letter from a solicitor in Sydney, Australia. My ex-partner died last month. In his will, he stipulated that I was to receive five thousand pounds. I've already made my reservation for a flight to New York!"

Infinite Intelligence is all-wise. It will always respond and react according to the nature of your request. Its ways are beyond finding out.

PRAYER OVERCOMES RACIAL PREJUDICE

When I was younger, I served in the army. Isaac G. was a member of my battalion. One day he told me, "I've always dreamed of becoming a doctor. I applied to medical school two years in a row, but I was turned down both times. I guess I have to give up my ambition."

"Why were you turned down?" I asked. "Did you have low grades in college?"

"Not at all," he replied. "My marks were way above average. And I know my professors gave me good recommendations. No, I'm convinced it was purely a matter of prejudice. The medical school already had too many students of my racial background, so they turned me down."

I had no way of knowing whether Isaac's conclusion was correct. I did know that in those days such things happened; they still do in some places. In any case, I could see that he was convinced of what he had said. I told him that Infinite Intelligence does not discriminate. It answers all people according to their belief.

We talked for a long time about the relationship of the conscious and subconscious mind. By the end of our discussion, Isaac began to see that his subconscious mind had the answer to his problem, if only he would turn the problem over to it.

I encouraged him to try an experiment. At night, as he was about to fall asleep, he was to imagine a medical diploma inscribed with his name and stating he was a fully qualified physician and surgeon. He was to take this diploma in his hand and feel the pride of accomplishment in having earned it. He worked to make his mental picture as real and natural as he could, to impress it on his subconscious mind.

One morning soon afterward, Isaac came looking for me. "I have a feeling that something is about to happen," he said. "Somehow, I don't think I'll be around here much longer." This was his subconscious mind telling him, "All is well."

Later that day, he was called in to see the commanding officer. Someone in Personnel had made note of Isaac's pre-med training in college and recommended that he take a screening exam. If he did well on it, he would be sent to medical school at the Army's expense. He had no trouble passing the examination and, as a result, soon began medical training. He let Infinite Intelligence open the door for him to become what his heart desired.

PRAYER OPENS PRISON DOORS

Some years ago, at the request of his family, I visited Gordon J., who was imprisoned in upstate New York.

"Are you here to tell me I'm free?" he demanded. "If you're not, then what good are you to me?"

"I'm here to help you find comfort in your situation," I replied.

"Oh, man, give me a break!" he burst out. "My situation! I'm locked up for the next five years for something I didn't even do. Guys who do things a lot worse than I ever did are out there, free as birds, living it up. Every minute of my life, I do nothing but pray for freedom. And you want me to find comfort in my situation? You're nuts!"

The biggest source of Gordon's bitterness was that he was in prison for a crime he hadn't committed. As we talked, however, he freely admitted that before being arrested, he had been carrying on a one-man war against society and against the Golden Rule.

"You were in prison long before they sent you here," I said. "You built your own prison—a psychological prison of hatred and envy. Even if you walk out of this place tomorrow, you'll carry that prison with you. But if you are willing to put those negative attitudes aside, you'll find real freedom even if you are still behind these walls."

I gave Gordon detailed instructions on how to change his mental attitude. He began to pray for those he hated, by affirming frequently, "God's love flows through them. I wish success and happiness and peace for all of them." He continued to do this many times a day. At night, before going to sleep, he imagined himself back home with his family. He visualized his little daughter in his arms and heard her voice saying, "I'm so glad you're home, Daddy."

Gordon did all this in his imagination. After a while he made it so real, natural, and vivid that it became a part of him. He had succeeded in impregnating his subconscious with the belief in freedom.

As he continued, he discovered that he no longer felt driven to pray for his freedom. This was a sure psychological sign that he had embodied the desire for freedom subjectively. He was at peace, and though he was behind bars, he knew subjectively that he was free. It was an inner knowing. Having realized his desire subjectively, he had no further compulsion to pray for it.

Some months later, I learned that Gordon had been released from prison. Friends who had never lost faith in him had uncovered new evidence that proved his innocence. A door to a new life opened for him.

HER PRAYER SAVED HIM FROM FINANCIAL DISASTER

Ramona S. was in constant attendance at the weekly lectures I gave on one of my books, *The Power of Your Subconscious Mind* (Paramus, NJ: Reward Books, 2000). After one of the sessions, she approached me and started to weep.

When she got her feelings under control again, she said, "I don't know what to do. Mike, my boyfriend, owns a computer store. It did so well for so long, and he was so proud of his success. Now, suddenly, he says he may lose the store."

"Why?" I asked. "What's the problem?"

She shook her head. "I don't know," she told me. "He

can't meet his bills, that's all. He may even lose his apartment and his car. Everything is tied up in the store. We were talking about getting married, but now . . . It isn't possible. I don't see any way out. The whole thing's hopeless."

"Ramona, what are you doing when you make statements like that?" I asked.

"Telling it like it is!" she said bitterly. "No, I know what you mean. I'm filling my subconscious mind with the thought of failure, right?"

"Right," I agreed. "And what *should* you do?"

"Reverse it," she replied. "That's what we all learned, isn't it? But how?"

"First, put yourself in a quiet, passive, receptive state of mind," I said. "Then fill yourself with the feeling that there is a way out for Mike and for you."

Every night, Ramona went to sleep dwelling on this wonderful truth: "I know there is a solution for us through the wisdom of my subconscious mind. I accept the way out now and the happy ending in divine order."

At my suggestion she built on this procedure, and three or four times daily she entered into the mood or feeling that there was a solution for her boyfriend.

In using this technique of prayer, Ramona was deliberately rejecting the evidence of her senses, including her "common sense." Instead, she looked to the wisdom of the subconscious for an answer.

Less than two weeks later, Mike called to tell her that a miracle had happened. He had just received an e-mail message from his most important supplier. The supplier had been inadvertantly overcharging Mike's store for more than two months. His account was not overdue; in fact, he had a substantial credit balance.

The answer to Mike's and Ramona's difficulty had come out of the blue, in response to her prayer of faith. The Bible says, *Before they call, I will answer; and while they are yet speaking, I will hear* (Isa. 65:24).

YOUR DAILY PRAYER

I know that no matter what the negation of yesterday was, my prayer or affirmation of truth will rise triumphantly over it today.

Today is God's day; it is a glorious day for me. I am full of peace, harmony, and joy. My faith is in the goodness of God, in the guidance of God, and in the love of God. I am absolutely convinced that my deeper mind receives the impression of my present thoughts, and I am irresistibly attracting into my experience all the good things my heart desires. I now place all my reliance, faith, and trust in the power and wisdom of God within me; I am at peace.

I hear the invitation of the God-Presence within me saying, *Come unto me, all ye that labour . . . and I will give you rest* (Matt. 11:28).

I rest in God; all is well.

POINTS TO REMEMBER

1. Prayer is always the solution. Prayer is a wish turned God-ward, and God answers you.

2. With God all things are possible. God is all-powerful and knows no opposition.

3. Complete and utter faith in God can save you from death.

4. Let divine love and peace enter your heart, and the past will be wiped out and remembered no more.

5. Changed attitudes change everything in your life, and your whole world magically transforms into the image and likeness of your dominant conviction.

6. In prayer, ignore your doubts and fears and acknowledge that Infinite Intelligence knows the way out and has the "know-how" of accomplishment.

7. Creative Intelligence, which is God in all people, is no respecter of persons, and it answers all people according to their beliefs.

8. Prayer opens prison doors when you are living in a psychological prison of hatred, envy, and vengeance.

9. There is always a way. Still the wheels of your mind and be aware that God knows the answer and, because God knows, you know. *I and my Father are one* (John 10:30).

10. *What things soever ye desire, when ye pray, believe that ye receive them, and ye shall have them* (Mark 11:24).

LAW 2

THE SECRET LAW
OF FAITH

Faith is a way of thinking, a mental attitude that gets results. The faith spoken of in the Bible is a conviction based on eternal laws and principles that never change. Faith is a fusion of your thought and feeling, or your mind and heart, that is so complete, inflexible, and impregnable that no external events or happenings can move you.

In the eleventh chapter of Mark, you can read a marvelous verse, the twenty-third, on the power of faith:

> *For verily I say unto you, That whosoever shall say unto this mountain* (your problem, difficulty), *Be thou removed* (that is, eradicated, dissolved), *and be thou cast into the sea* (that means the "sea" of your subconscious, where the healing or solution takes place and problems disappear); *and shall not doubt in his heart* (the heart means your subconscious mind; in other words, your conscious thought and subjective feeling must agree), *but shall believe that those things which he saith shall come to pass; he shall have whatsoever he saith.*

These great truths are very explicit. There is a power and a wisdom within you that can lift you up out of poverty and sickness, reveal to you the answer to your prayer, and set you on the high road to happiness, peace of mind, joy, and harmonious relationships with all people and with the whole world.

FAITH-POWER WORKS WONDERS

Some years ago, while flying to the East Coast, I sat next to a man who told me that he was a member of a sales force for a large biochemical firm that had two hundred representatives in the field. His name was William B. When he asked what my line of work was, I described myself as a motivational speaker.

"I wish I'd known you a few weeks ago," he replied. "I could have used a little motivation. I still could, for that matter."

"What's the problem?" I asked.

"Well, the manager of my division suddenly announced she was taking early retirement," he said. "Next thing I know, *her* boss, whom I know only from meetings and conferences, calls me in. He asks me to take her place."

"Congratulations," I said.

"Not so fast," he said, holding up a hand like a traffic cop. "I said no. I turned it down. I've been kicking myself ever since, but that's what I did."

I studied his face. I could detect signs of an inner struggle there. "I see," I said. "What were your reasons?"

He gave a short, bitter laugh. "Oh, I had a lot of them, but they were all phony. The fact is, I was scared. No, terrified. How could I possibly handle that kind of responsibility? I was sure I'd make a total fool of myself. So instead, guess what? I turned down the greatest opportunity that's ever likely to come my way. Talk about making a fool of myself!"

It was Shakespeare who wrote, "Our doubts are traitors, making us lose the good we oft might win, by fearing to attempt." William had profound faith in the negative, in his own inadequacy and inability to take on a promotion and to face life.

William and I talked for the rest of the flight, and we met again the next day in New York. At my suggestion, he committed himself to making the following affirmation several times a day:

> I am redirecting my thought and feeling. I do not need more faith, I need to use and apply the faith I have in the right way. I know that my subconscious mind reacts according to what I believe about myself. I have faith in the indwelling God, and I know that God is guiding me and directing me. I was born to succeed. Infinite Intelligence reveals to me a new opportunity. I know that I am full of confidence and poise. I have faith in all things good, and I live in the joyous expectancy of the best.

As William began to identify mentally and emotionally with these ideas, his approach to his job and his approach to life changed. Not long afterward, he was offered a managerial post in another division of his firm. This time he accepted it with joy in his heart. This is the magic power of faith.

EVERYONE HAS FAITH

Everyone has faith in something. Some have faith in failure, sickness, accidents, and misfortune. When you hear exhortations to have faith, you must remember that you already have faith. The question is, how are you using it—constructively or negatively?

Our mental attitudes and beliefs, which represent our faith, make our own heaven and hell. What is your faith? The noblest, grandest, and highest faith is based on eternal principles that never change. Have faith in the creative law of your own mind, in the goodness of God and in all things good, a joyous expectancy of the best, and a firm belief inscribed in your heart that Infinite Intelligence will lead you out of your difficulty and show you the way. Have a firm conviction in the power of God to solve your problems and to heal you. Have faith in the invisible Intelligence within you, which created you and is all-powerful, and which enables you to walk over the waters of fear, doubt, worry, and imaginary dangers of all kinds.

FAITH IN THE INVISIBLE

Paul said, *Faith is the substance of things hoped for, the evidence of things not seen* (Heb. 11:1).

All great scientists, mystics, poets, artists, and inventors are gifted and are possessed of an abiding faith and trust in the invisible powers within. The scientists and inventors have faith in the possibility of the execution of "the idea." The idea of the Internet, though invisible, was real in the mind of the inventor; the idea of an automobile was real in the mind of Henry Ford; the idea of a new structure is real in the mind of the architect. The idea of this book exists in my mind, and its pages come forth from the invisible ideas, thoughts, imagery, and beliefs that inhabit my mind.

You must appreciate the fact that your desire, idea, dream, new play, book, script, trip, enterprise, or adventure are all real in your mind, though invisible. To know that your idea is real, that it has form, shape, and substance on the mental plane, and that it is as real as your hand on the objective plane, gives you scientific faith. This knowledge enables you to walk over the waters of confusion, strife, and fear to a place of conviction deep in your subconscious mind. Whatever is conveyed to your subconscious is projected on the screen of space. It is in this way that your ideas become objectified.

HOW HIS FAITH TRIUMPHED

While lecturing in San Francisco, I met Arthur R., the general manager of a large corporation. He confided to me that he had lost confidence in himself. He was very unhappy and dejected over the way his career was going.

"I report to two people," he explained, "the executive vice president and the CEO. Both of them keep opposing me. Whatever I suggest, they're against it automatically. Between them, they are driving the firm into the ground. Before long, my stock options will be worthless. I'll have wasted five years of my life. And the worst part is, I have absolutely no faith in my ability to do anything about it."

"You're right about at least one thing," I told him. "The worst part of your situation *is* your lack of faith in yourself. Unless you are willing to put your confidence in the invisible powers within you, whatever you do is going to go badly."

"Invisible powers!" he scoffed. "I'm sorry. I don't mean to belittle your beliefs. I'm sure you're very sincere. But as for me, I believe in what I can see, hear, touch, taste, or smell. I don't have room in my system for mystical ideas."

I smiled. "I understand. Many people feel the same way. But *where* do they feel that way? Can you pin down the location of their skepticism?"

"Why, it's in their minds, I suppose," he replied. "You're going to ask me where my mind is. All right. I have to admit, I don't know exactly."

"But you know you have one," I said.

"Unless I've lost it," he joked. "No, I see your point."

"Do you have children?" I asked. He nodded. "Do you love them? Can you *see* that love? Or only its effects in the world? It is the same with the Infinite Intelligence that is within you and every person. We cannot see it, we cannot locate it with a CAT scan of the brain, but we can see its effects in the world."

As we continued to talk, Arthur realized an important truth. In order to advance in business and to have peace of mind and success, he had to anchor himself to a wisdom and a power that transcended his intellect. He had to get in touch with that which is substantial and eternal. He made a deliberate decision to unite mentally and emotionally with the inner power lodged in his subconscious mind.

At my suggestion, he resolved to focus on the following prayer several times daily:

All those who work in our corporation are spiritual, wonderful, God-like links in the chain of its growth, welfare, and prosperity. I radiate good will in my thoughts, words, and deeds to all those I work with. I am full of love and good will for the CEO and the vice president of our company. Infinite Intelligence makes all decisions through me. There is only right action taking place in my life. I send the thought messengers of peace, love, joy, and harmony before me to the office, and the peace of God reigns supreme in the minds and hearts of all those in the company, including myself. I now go forth into a new day full of faith, confidence, and trust.

Arthur repeated the above prayer slowly four or five times daily, feeling the truth behind the words. He poured life, love, truth, and confidence into the words, and they sank deep down into his subconscious mind. When fearful or angry thoughts came into his mind during the day, he would say, "God's peace fills my soul." After a while, all the harmful thoughts ceased to come, and peace came into his mind.

I later received a letter from Arthur. At the end of two weeks, the CEO and the vice president met with him privately. Each shook hands with him and said that the organization could not get along without his creative energies. His faith was restored. He knew that, as a conscious individual, with the capability of free choice, he had the power to choose success, harmony, and good will, and to rise above all circumstances and conditions. Therefore, he was not under the dominion of externalities or the impressions of the senses.

SHE CHANGED HER FAITH

Rebecca G. was a young woman with very special talents as an actor and singer. She came to me because she was having great difficulty in getting any work in television or the movies. She went constantly to auditions, but she had been turned down so often that she feared she was developing a rejection complex.

"It's not really surprising," she said. "There are lots of actresses out there who are more beautiful than I am. I guess that's the reason they get chosen and I don't."

"That's one possibility" I replied. "But you know, there is a law of mind that states that supply and demand are two aspects of one thing. What you are seeking is also seeking you. If you place your faith in Infinite Intelligence, it will direct you to your true place."

"How can I do that?" she asked. "Please, help me!"

"What you must do first is put aside your faith in rejection," I explained. "Believe in acceptance, recognition, and true expression. Understand that whatever your mind can imagine and feel to be true, you can also realize."

Rebecca began to follow a new discipline. Twice a day, she quieted the activity of her mind and removed all tension from her body by simply talking to it and telling it to relax. She knew that if she ordered it in this way, it had to obey. In that quiet, receptive, peaceful state, she focused her attention completely on an imaginary movie contract in her hand. She felt the joy and reality of it all. She willed the contract to become a reality. She became identified with the imaginary picture of the contract in her mind, and she had faith that what she imagined and believed must come to pass. She changed her mind—her state of faith— and according to her faith was it done unto her. Before the end of the month, she auditioned for a new television series and was given an important part.

And calleth those things which be not as though they were (Rom. 4:17).

HIS FAITH MADE HIM WHOLE

I was giving a series of lectures in Bombay, India when I met Basil F., an Englishman who had great trouble with his legs in the wake of an automobile accident. After a long confinement at home and intensive physical therapy, he was able to walk, but only with great difficulty and with the aid of a cane.

"What would you do if you were healed?" I asked him.

"What wouldn't I!" he replied. "I would certainly swim, golf, play polo, and go climbing in the Alps. I used to do that every year."

That was the sort of answer I was seeking. I told Basil in the simplest way possible how to achieve the perfect use of his legs again. The first step was to imagine he was doing the things he ordinarily would have done before his accident.

I suggested that he sit in his study for fifteen or twenty minutes, three times a day, and imagine that he was playing polo. He was to assume the mental mood of actually performing the role of a polo player. In other words, he had to play the role of an actor, as every actor participates in the role he or she characterizes and dramatizes.

Basil carried out these instructions carefully. He felt himself playing polo. Note carefully that he did not *see* himself playing polo; that would have been an illusion projected outside of himself and viewed from a distance. No, he *actualized* the state by living the drama in his mind. He made it so real and so vivid in his mind that the tangibility of the mallet and the naturalness of the touch of the polo pony became real to him.

At noon he would quiet his mind, still his body, and practically feel his mountaineering clothes on him. He would imagine and physically sense that he was climbing in the Alps; he felt the cold air on his face and heard the voices of his former climbing partners. He lived the drama and felt the solidity and hardness of the rocks.

At night, before going to sleep, he would play an imaginary round of golf. He would hold the club, touch the ball with his hand, put it in place, and tee off. He would swing his club and delight in watching the ball sail straight up the fairway toward the green. He got into the mood of playing a good game, and he went off to sleep feeling very satisfied and happy about his imaginary experiences of the day.

Within two months this man's legs had improved wonderfully. He went on to do all the things he had imagined he would do. Gradually, his imaginary pictures impregnated the deeper layers of his subconscious mind where the healing power is. There was a reflex action that corresponded to his mental image and feeling. His subconscious mind faithfully reproduced what he had impressed upon it.

FAITH IS YOUR MIND

You are really invisible. Others do not see your motives, feelings, faith, confidence, dreams, aspirations, longings, or the Life Principle within you. When you recall this, you know that you are invulnerable, invincible, eternal, and immortal. You are not a slave of conditions or a victim of circumstance. The Divine Life lives, moves, and has its being in you, and you live, move, and have your being in this same Divine Life.

Everything in your world is a manifestation of your faith in the unseen. This Omnipotent Presence called God is responsive to your thought and feeling. For example, if you claim, "I am strong and powerful," you will become strong and robust. Your faith is something you become, because you manifest and objectify in your world what you really believe about yourself.

Faith without works is dead (James 2:26). In other words, you will see the works of faith in your mind, body, and affairs. The works of your faith appear in your business or profession, in your home, in the functions of your body, and in all your undertakings. The fruits of faith are health, happiness, peace, love, good will, abundance, security, poise, balance, serenity, and tranquillity.

HER FAITH
IN INFINITE INTELLIGENCE

I was recently at a dinner at the house of friends in Los Angeles. I got to talking with a young woman named Colleen M. When she mentioned that she was in computer graphics, I said, "That's a very active field these days, isn't it?"

"It certainly is," she replied. "A little too active sometimes! As a matter of fact, I just had to deal with a really difficult problem. An Internet-related company in New York offered me a job. It would have meant a good deal more money than I'm getting where I am, but of course I would have had to move to New York."

"How did you decide what to do?" I asked, intrigued.

"I went off to one of my favorite spots, up in the hills, and quieted my mind," she replied. "Then I asked myself,

'How would I be feeling right now if I had just made the right decision about this?'"

"And what did yourself answer?" I asked.

She smiled. "Myself told me I would feel wonderful. I would be happy and confident about my decision."

Act as though I am, and I will be. Colleen had discovered this truth in her own life. She acted as though she had made the right decision, knowing that the creative Principle of Life is one of love and responsiveness and that it loved her and cared for her. She began to say, "Isn't it wonderful! Isn't it wonderful!" over and over again. That night, she lulled herself to sleep in the feeling, "It is wonderful."

That night she had a dream. She was back at her favorite spot, gazing off toward the distant coastline. Suddenly she realized that the wind in the bushes was speaking words. It said, "Stand still! Stand still!" She woke up. She knew that she had just heard the inner voice of intuition.

"What did you do?" I inquired.

"The only thing I *could* do," she told me. "I listened to my inner voice. I turned down the New York offer. And it's a very good thing I did. You may not believe this, but I heard today that the firm just let go about thirty percent of its people. If I'd moved there, I might be out of a job now."

I the Lord (the law of your subconscious mind) *will make myself known unto him in a vision, and will speak unto him in a dream* (Num. 12:6).

SERVE YOURSELF WITH FAITH-POWER

1. Faith is a mental attitude that commands and gets results.

2. You do not need more faith. You have plenty of faith, but you must use it constructively. Give it purposeful direction. Have faith in health, success, peace, and happiness.

3. Everyone has faith in something. Where is your faith? Real faith is based on eternal principles and the values of life that never change.

4. Faith is invisible. It is the evidence of things not seen. Scientists have great faith, because they believe in the possibility of the execution of the ideas in their minds.

5. You can't see your mind, your life, or your feeling of love. You can't see faith, either, but you can anchor your mind on the invisible power within you, which is substantial, eternal, and all-powerful.

6. Change your faith in failure and rejection into faith in acceptance, recognition, and successful living.

7. Have faith in the Healing Power. Imagine and feel that you are now doing all the things you would do were you made whole.

8. Your faith is your mind, and in your deeper mind dwells the omnipotence of God, which responds to your thought and feeling. This is why you can overcome all circumstances and conditions.

9. Mentally act and feel the way you would act and feel were your prayer answered, and you will find that the magic power of faith will work wonders in your life.

LAW 3

THE MIRACULOUS LAW OF HEALING

There is only one healing power. It has been called by many names. They include God, the Infinite Healing Presence, Nature, Divine Love, and the Life Principle. All of these, different as they may seem, refer to the same cosmic truth. The knowledge of this power goes back into the dim recesses of the past. An inscription has been found written over ancient temples. It reads, *The doctor dresses the wound, and God heals the patient.*

The healing presence of God is within you. No psychologist, minister, doctor, surgeon, priest, or psychiatrist heals anyone. When a surgeon removes a tumor, what this really does is remove a block to make way for the healing power of God. Similarly, a psychologist or psychiatrist works to remove mental blocks and encourages the patient to adopt a new mental attitude that tends to release the healing presence, flowing through the patient as harmony, health, and peace. A minister asks you to forgive yourself and others and to get in tune with the Infinite by letting the healing power of love, peace, and good will flow through your subconscious mind, thereby cleansing all the negative patterns that may be lodged there.

This infinite healing presence of life, which Jesus called "Father," is the healing agent in all diseases, whether mental, emotional, or physical.

This miraculous healing power in your subconscious mind, if scientifically directed, can heal your mind, body, and affairs of all disease and impediments. This healing power will respond to you regardless of your race, creed, or color. It does not care whether you belong to any church or whether you have any creedal affiliations or not. You have had hundreds of healings since you were a child. You can recall how this healing presence brought curative results to cuts, burns, bruises, contusions, and sprains—and these miracles happened without your conscious effort or knowledge of *how* they happened.

HEALED OF SPIRIT-VOICES

A few years ago, a young man named Dean W., a student at a local university, came to see me in deep distress.

"I think I am going crazy," he told me. "I am constantly hearing spirit-voices. They won't let me alone. They keep telling me to do terrible things. When I try to read the Bible or other spiritual books, they come up close and shout obscenities in my ear. They are demons with supernatural power, and I'm afraid they are gaining control over me."

What Dean did not realize was that he was experiencing the faculty of clairaudience. He had the power to hear things that are not physically present. All people have this ability to some degree, but in him it was unusually strong. Because he did not understand the cause of the phenomenon, he began to think it was due to evil spirits. His superstitious beliefs caused him to ascribe it to departed spirits. Through constant worry, he developed a monomania for the subject. His subconscious mind, dominated and controlled by an all-potent but false suggestion, gradually took over control and mastery of his objective faculties, and his reason abdicated its throne. He was what you would call mentally unbalanced, as is anyone who allows false beliefs to obtain ascendancy.

"You know, Dean," I explained, "your subconscious mind has tremendous power. It can be influenced either negatively or positively. What you must do is be sure that you influence it only positively, constructively, and harmoniously. Otherwise, your complaint may well grow worse, as your subconscious mind responds to the bad suggestions you are flooding it with."

The explanation I gave Dean made a profound impression on him. Before he left, I wrote out a prayer for him to repeat for ten or fifteen minutes, three or four times a day:

> God's love, peace, harmony, and wisdom flood my mind and heart. I love the truth, I hear the truth, and I know the truth that God is Love, and his love surrounds me, enfolds me, and enwraps me. God's river of peace floods my mind, and I give thanks for my freedom.

Dean repeated this prayer slowly, quietly, reverently, and with deep feeling, especially before sleep. By identifying himself with harmony and peace, he brought about a rearrangement of the thought patterns and imagery of his mind, and a healing followed. He brought about the healing of his mind by repetition of these truths, coupled with faith and expectancy.

I remembered him in my own devotions as well. Night and morning, I recited the following prayer:

> Dean is thinking rightly. He is reflecting Divine Wisdom and Divine Intelligence in all his ways. His mind is the perfect mind of God, unchanging and eternal. He hears the voice of God, which is the inner voice of peace and love. God's river of peace governs his mind, and he is full of wisdom, poise, balance, and understanding. Whatever is vexing him is leaving him now, and I pronounce him free and at peace.

I meditated on these truths each night and morning, until my mind was filled with a sense of peace and harmony. At the end of a week, this young man was completely free and at peace.

SHE WASN'T EXPECTED TO LIVE

Mary B., who often attended my lectures, brought Pamela P. to speak to me. Pamela's face was twisted with terrible distress. Before I could ask what was wrong, she burst out, "I shouldn't be here! My little girl may be dying at this very minute!" She started to cry hysterically.

Mary explained. Pamela's four-year-old was in the hospital with a very high fever of mysterious origin. The doctors feared some variety of encephalitis. They were administering antibiotics, but so far the child's fever was not responding.

"I feel so bad for her," Mary continued. "Nothing seems to go right in her life." Pamela and her husband had broken up less than a month earlier, after years of strife. Since then, Pamela had become increasingly distressed and agitated.

Once Pamela regained a measure of calm, I said, "You have to understand that children are very much at the mercy of their parents. They soak up the dominant mental atmosphere and emotional climate of those around them. They have not yet reached the age of reason, when they can take control of their own thoughts, emotions, and reactions to life."

"What do you mean?" Pamela demanded.

"The doctors who are treating your daughter will do everything medical science can do," I said. "I'm sure of that. But you can do more. You can make a conscious decision to become more at ease with yourself. I suggest you begin by reading the Twenty-third Psalm. Pray for guidance and for peace and harmony. In particular, ask for help in giving up the resentment and inner rage you feel toward your husband."

"If you knew how he's treated me—," she began.

"Do those negative feelings mean more to you than the health of your child?" I asked.

"No, of course not!" she protested.

"Then strive to give them up," I continued. "Pour out love and good will toward him. Abandon your rage and anger, which communicate themselves subjectively to your daughter. Try it. Just as resentment feeds resentment, love feeds love."

Pamela returned to her child's bedside. After meditating for a long time on the Twenty-third Psalm, she began to pray for her daughter:

> Spirit, which is God, is the life of my child. Spirit has no temperature; it is never sick or feverish. The peace of God flows through my child's mind and body. The harmony, health, love, and perfection of God are made manifest in every atom of my child's body now. She is relaxed and at ease, poised, serene, and calm. I am now stirring up the gift of God within her, and all is well.

She repeated this prayer every hour for several hours. As night fell, she saw an amazing change in her child, who woke up and said, "Mommy, where's my dolly? I'm so hungry!"

The nurse confirmed that the child's fever had broken. What had happened? The fever left the little girl because the mother was no longer feverish or agitated in her mind. Her mood of peace, harmony, and love was instantaneously felt by the child, and a corresponding reaction was produced.

THE NATURAL-BORN HEALER

Sometimes we are told that a particular person is a "natural-born healer." This is superstition. The truth is that we are all natural-born healers. The reason is simple: The healing presence of God is within all people. All of us can contact it with our thoughts. It responds to all. It is omnipresent. It is the life of all things.

DEGREES OF FAITH

There are different degrees of faith. There is the person who, through faith, heals someone's chronic ache. There is another who heals a deep-seated, so-called incurable malignancy. It is as easy for the healing presence of God to heal a tubercular lung as it is to heal a cut on your finger. There is no great or small in the God that made us all; there is no big or little, no hard or easy. Omnipotence is within all people. The prayers of the healer who lays a hand on another in order to induce a healing simply appeal to the cooperation of the patient's unconscious. Whether the patient knows it or not, whether you ascribe it to divine intercession or not, if the patient's subconscious becomes impregnated with the idea of health, a response takes place. For according to the patient's faith is it done unto you.

A CASE OF PALSY

An old friend of mine in New York City, Howard D., suffered from palsy and tremors. Sometimes he would find himself suddenly unable to move. He would be frozen to the spot, even in the middle of a busy street. His doctor prescribed medications that gave him some relief from his symptoms, but they could not relieve his constant feeling of fear, panic, and foreboding. Those feelings were wearing him down.

When Howard appealed to me for help, I laid out a procedure for him to follow. My first goal was to get him to see that there was a miraculous healing power within him that had made his body and that could heal it. I urged him to ponder the fifth chapter of Luke, verses 18–24, and a related passage, Mark 2:5–11, where Jesus said to the man with palsy: *Son, thy sins be forgiven thee . . . I say unto thee, Arise, and take up thy bed, and go thy way into thine house.*

Howard read these verses avidly. He was deeply moved by them, because he so much identified with the man in the Bible story. I explained to him that the couch or bed mentioned in the Bible means the bed in which a person lies in his own mind. The paralyzed man in the Bible undoubtedly was lying down amid thoughts of fear, doubt, condemnation, guilt, and superstition. These thoughts paralyze the mind and body.

We are told that Jesus healed the man of palsy by forgiving him his sins. To sin is to miss the mark, the goal of health, happiness, and peace. You forgive yourself when you identify mentally and emotionally with your ideal and continue to do so until it gels within you as a conviction or subjective embodiment. You sin when you think negatively or if you resent, hate, condemn, or engage in fear or worry. You are always sinning when you deviate or turn away from your announced goal or aim in life, which should always be peace, harmony, wisdom, and perfect health—the life more abundant.

Howard admitted to me that he was full of hatred toward a brother who had double-crossed him years ago in a financial deal. He was also full of guilt and self-condemnation. He came to realize that, like the paralytic in the Bible, he could not be healed until his sins had been canceled by simply forgiving himself and his brother.

Howard turned to the healing presence of God within him. He affirmed boldly:

> I fully and freely forgive myself for harboring negative and destructive thoughts, and I resolve to purify my mind from now on. I surrender and release my brother to God. Wherever he is, I sincerely wish for him health, happiness, and all the blessings of God. I am now aligned with the Infinite Healing Power, and I feel divine love flowing through every atom of my being. I know that God's love is now permeating and saturating my entire body, making me whole and perfect. I sense the peace that passeth understanding. My body is a temple of the living God. God is in his holy temple and I am free.

As he meditated on these truths, Howard gradually became reconditioned to health and harmony. As he changed his mind, he changed his body. Changed attitudes change everything. Today, Howard walks joyously and freely, completely healed.

SHE HEALED HER WITHERED HAND

"I simply don't get it," Irene R. told me. She had come up to speak to me after a meeting. "Last week I was let go from my job at a small publishing house. It was the publisher who dropped the bomb on me, and she said such a peculiar thing. She said, 'You're just like the man in the Bible with the withered hand.' What on earth was she talking about? There's nothing at all wrong with my hands!"

"You have to understand," I said. "In the Bible, principles are often personified. In other words, the person in an account often stands for something else as well. This is a way to make portrayal and interaction more vivid and forceful."

"Okay," Irene said. "I've studied literature. I know about symbolism. But what's with the withered hand?"

"The hand is a symbol of power, direction, and effectiveness," I replied. "With your hand, you fashion, mold, direct, and design. Symbolically, a person who has a withered hand has an inferiority complex and feels guilty and inadequate, or is a defeatist. Such a person does not function efficiently and is not expressing his or her God-given powers."

Irene's face changed. "Now I see. It's true—my dreams and ambitions have withered. But how could it be otherwise? There is no way I can bring them to pass. Isn't that what it means to grow up? To give up childish dreams?"

"No!" I said emphatically. "To give up your dreams is not to grow up, it is to start to die! When you let your wonderful ideas die aborning in your mind, you are stagnating, dying on the vine. You must stretch forth your hand, by enlarging your concept and estimation of yourself. What is it you most want to achieve? Form a picture in your mind. See yourself accomplishing your dream."

"I love publishing," Irene said softly. "What I really want to do is find ways to give voice to people who are silenced. If I could find a way . . ."

I suggested that Irene meditate on this goal, that she visualize herself speaking with some of the people she wanted to help and telling them that their words would be heard by millions of people. She began to affirm frequently:

> I can do all things through the God-power, which strengthens, guides, controls, and directs me. I realize that I am going where my vision is. I now turn with faith and confidence to the Infinite Intelligence within me, knowing that I am directed by an inner wisdom. I know in my heart that the God-power flows through the patterns of thought and imagery in my mind, and I am under a divine compulsion to accomplish my dreams.

A few months later I received a note from Irene. She and a friend had written a film script that drew on the stories Irene had collected from people in her neighborhood. The script had won a prize that included substantial financing for the film to be made from it. The words of the people Irene wanted to help would indeed be heard by millions.

HOW THE HOPELESS CASE WAS HEALED

Jesus commanded the dead man: *And he said, Young man, I say unto thee, Arise. And he that was dead sat up, and began to speak* (Luke 7:14–15).

When the Bible recounts that the dead man sat up and began to speak, what does that mean? It means that when your prayer is answered, you speak in a new tongue of joyous health. You give forth an inner radiance. Your dead hopes and desires speak when you bear witness to your inner beliefs and assumptions.

Patrick O. is a distant relative of mine. A few years ago, his brother Michael asked me to come with him to the hospital to visit Patrick. Patrick was in a coma and suffering from kidney failure. The doctors pronounced his condition hopeless.

Patrick was unconscious when we got to his room. He showed no sign of knowing we were there. I pulled a chair close to his bedside. I knew he was a devout Catholic. In a soft voice, I said to him, "Patrick, Jesus is here with you. You see Him. He is putting His hand out. At this moment He is laying His hand upon you." I repeated this several times, slowly, gently, and positively.

Patrick's eyes suddenly opened. He looked from me to his brother and said, "I've had a visitor. Jesus was here. I know I am healed. I shall live."

What had happened? A miracle? Not in the sense that it cannot be explained, no. Patrick's subconscious mind had accepted my statement that Jesus was there. It projected that thought-form. He believed that Jesus was there in the flesh and that He had placed His hands upon him.

The faith that was kindled in the subconscious mind of my Catholic relative was based on his firm belief that Jesus had come to heal him. It was this belief that was the healing factor. It is always done unto us according to our faith, mental conviction, or even blind belief. Patrick's subconscious mind was amenable to my suggestion. His deeper mind received and acted upon the idea I had planted in his mind. In a sense, you could call what happened the resurrection of the dead. It was the resurrection of his health and vitality. According to his belief was it done unto him.

BLIND FAITH AND TRUE FAITH

True faith is based on the knowledge of the way your conscious and subconscious minds function and on the combined harmonious functioning of these two levels of mind scientifically directed. Blind faith is healing without any scientific understanding whatsoever of the forces involved. If a person believes that something is the holy bone of a saint, and that it has healing power, the fact that it is really a cleverly molded piece of plastic does not make any difference. It is not the bone that heals, but the fact that it has moved people's minds from fear to faith.

In all instances—regardless of the technique, process, incantation, or invocation offered to saints and spirits—it is the subconscious mind that does the healing. Whatever you believe is operative instantly in your subconscious mind.

Be like the eight-year-old girl in our Sunday school. She had suffered for several days from a painful eye irritation. The eyedrops the pediatrician prescribed did not seem to help. She prayed, "God, you made my eyes. You can heal them. How about right now? Thank you." Because of her simplicity, spontaneity, and child's faith in God, she had a remarkable healing. *Go, and do thou likewise* (Luke 10:37).

HOW TO GIVE
A SPIRITUAL TREATMENT

A spiritual treatment is turning to the Indwelling God and reminding yourself of His peace, harmony, wholeness, beauty, boundless love, and limitless power. Know that God loves you and cares for you. As you pray this way, the fear will gradually fade away. If you pray about a heart condition, do not think of the organ as diseased. This would not be spiritual thinking. Thoughts are things. Your spiritual thought takes form as cells, tissues, nerves, and organs. To think of a damaged heart or high blood pressure tends to suggest more of what you already have. Stop dwelling on symptoms, organs, or any part of the body. Turn your mind to God and His love. Feel and know that there is only one Healing Presence and Power, and accept this corollary: There is no power to challenge the action of God.

Quietly and lovingly affirm that the uplifting, healing, strengthening power of the Healing Presence is flowing through you, making you whole. Know and feel that the harmony, beauty, and life of God manifest themselves in you as strength, peace, vitality, wholeness, and right action. Achieve a clear realization of this, and the damaged heart or other diseased organ will be cured in the light of God's love.

Glorify God in your body (1 Cor. 6:20).

VERY PROFITABLE POINTERS

1. The healing power of God is within you. Remove any mental block and let the healing power flow through you.

2. Monomaniacs are people who permit their minds to be dominated and controlled by an all-potent but false suggestion.

3. When a parent is agitated and seething with inner turmoil and rage, this negative emotion is communicated to the subconscious of the child and can cause illness. Let God's river of peace flood the mind and heart; then the child's illness will abate and harmony will be restored.

4. All of us are natural-born healers, because the Infinite Healing Presence is within us and we can contact it with our thoughts and beliefs.

5. The miraculous healing power that made your body knows how to heal it. It knows all the processes and functions of your body. Trust the healing power, and accept a healing now.

6. You can recondition yourself to health and harmony as you meditate frequently on harmony, vitality, wholeness, beauty, and perfection.

7. In the Bible, principles are personified as persons in order to make portrayal and interaction vivid and forceful. You can overcome a feeling of inferi-

ority by joining up with God and by sensing that even one person with God is a majority.

8. There are no incurable diseases. There are incurable people who believe they can't be healed. According to their belief is it done unto them.

9. Faith healing is healing without any scientific understanding of the forces involved. Spiritual mind healing is the combined and harmonious functioning of your conscious and subconscious mind, scientifically directed for a specific purpose. In all instances, it is the subconscious mind that heals, regardless of the technique or process used.

HOW YOU CAN FACE THE WORD *INCURABLE* IN YOUR OWN LIFE

Don't let the word *incurable* frighten you. Realize that you are dealing with the Creative Intelligence that made your body. Some people may say that a healing is impossible, but be assured that this infinite Healing Presence is instantly available. You can always draw on its power through the creative law of your own mind. Make use of this power now and perform miracles in your life. Remember that a miracle cannot prove that which is impossible; it is a confirmation of that which is possible, for *with God all things are possible* (Matt. 19:26). *I will restore health unto thee, and I will heal thee of thy wounds, saith the Lord* (Jer. 30:17).

The word *Lord* in the Bible means the creative law of your mind. There is a deep-lying, healing principle that permeates the entire universe, that flows through your mental patterns, images, and choices, and objectifies them in form. You can bring into your life anything you wish through this infinite healing principle that operates through your own mind.

You can use this universal healing principle for any particular purpose. It is not confined to healing of the mind or body. It is the same principle that attracts to you the ideal husband or wife, helps you to prosper in business, finds for you your true place in life, and reveals answers to your most difficult problems. Through the correct application of this principle, you can become a great musician, physician, or diplomat. You can use it to bring harmony where discord exists, peace where there is pain, joy in place of sadness, and abundance in place of poverty.

HEALING OF DROPSY

I have known John G. for many years. He always struck me as someone who was not only very religious, but completely free of any ill will or resentment toward others. The last time I visited London, I arranged to meet him. I could hardly recognize him. His face and body were badly swollen, and in his eyes I saw a sad mixture of fatigue and fear.

When I asked how he was, he said, "Not really well, actually. I'm suffering from dropsy. Fluids accumulate in the tissues. The doctors don't use the term any more. They call what I have edema and say it may be a symptom of a heart problem. But for me it's dropsy and always will be. I saw my father die of it, you know."

"No, I didn't," I replied. "That must have been very difficult for you."

"Oh, yes, it made quite an impression," he said. "The treatment in those days was to put a large needle into his abdomen and try to draw off the fluid. Rather painful, and as far as I could tell, quite useless. I think it was at that moment that I became convinced the same thing would happen to me, that I too would contract dropsy. Quite rightly, as it turned out."

"John, have you ever heard of Dr. Phineas Parkhurst Quimby of Maine?" I asked.

He shook his head. "I'm quite sure I haven't. I would not easily forget such a marvelous name. Who is he, and why do you ask?"

I explained. "More than a century ago, Dr. Quimby set forth a simple and wonderful psychological truth. He said that if you believe something, it will become manifest, whether you are consciously thinking of it or not. You have believed all your life that you would develop this disease. Why should it surprise you that in the end you have?"

"Are you saying that my belief created my disease?" he asked in a troubled voice.

"Exactly," I replied. "Your lifelong fear is a perversion of the truth. It has no real power, because there is no principle behind disease. There is a principle of health, but none of disease; a principle of abundance, but none of poverty; a principle of honesty, but none of deceit; a principle of beauty, but none of ugliness. Your mind can be used negatively or positively. Unfortunately, up to this point, you have used it negatively."

"But if I change?" he asked. After a long, thoughtful pause, he continued. "The Healing Presence that made me must still be within me. But my disease-soaked thoughts have kept it from making me whole. What I must do is find a way to rearrange my mind to conform to the divine pattern of harmony, health, and wholeness. Can you help me?"

Together, John and I developed a spiritual therapy for him, and he put it into effect. Before going to sleep each night, he affirmed, with feeling and with deep meaning behind each word:

> The Healing Presence is now going to work, transforming, healing, restoring, and controlling all processes of my body according to its wisdom and divine nature. My entire system is cleansed, purified, and quickened by the vitalizing energy of God. Divine circulation, assimilation, and elimination operate in my mind and body. The joy of the Lord is my abiding strength. I am made whole in every way, and I give thanks.

John repeated this prayer every night for about thirty days. At the end of that time, his mind had achieved a conviction of health. On his next visit to his physician, he was told he had made a complete recovery.

STEPS IN HEALING

The first step in healing is not to be afraid of the manifest condition—from this very moment. The second step is to realize that the condition is only the product of past thinking, which will have no more power to continue its existence. The third step is to mentally exalt the miraculous healing power of God within you.

This procedure will instantly stop the production of all mental poisons in you or in the person for whom you are praying. Live in the embodiment of your desire, and your thought and feeling will soon be made manifest. Do not allow yourself to be swayed by human opinion and worldly fears, but live emotionally in the belief that it is God in action in your mind and body.

SPIRITUAL BLINDNESS

Millions of people are psychologically and spiritually "blind." They do not recognize that they become what they think all day long. People are spiritually and mentally blind when they are hateful, resentful, or envious of others. They do not know that they are actually secreting mental poisons that work to destroy them.

So many people constantly say that there is no way to solve their problems, that their situations are hopeless. Such an attitude is the result of spiritual blindness. We begin to see spiritually and mentally when we gain a new understanding of our mental powers and develop a conscious awareness that the wisdom and intelligence in our subconscious can solve all our problems.

Everyone should become aware of the interrelationship and interaction between the conscious and subconscious minds. Those who were once blind to these truths will, after careful introspection, begin to see the vision of health, wealth, happiness, and peace of mind that can be theirs through the correct application of the laws of mind.

VISION IS SPIRITUAL, ETERNAL, AND INDESTRUCTIBLE

We do not create vision. Instead, we manifest or release it. We see *through* the eye, not with it. The retina of the eye is stimulated by light waves from objects in space; through the optic nerve, the impulses are carried to the brain. When the inner light, or intelligence, meets the outer light in this manner, by a process of interpretation, we see.

Your eyes symbolize divine love and a delight in the ways of God, as well as a hunger and thirst for God's truth. Your right eye symbolizes right thought and right action. The left eye symbolizes God's love and wisdom. Think right and radiate good will to all, and you will focus perfectly.

Receive thy sight . . . And immediately he received his sight, and followed him, glorifying God (Luke 18:42–43).

SPECIAL PRAYER FOR EYES AND EARS

I am the Lord that healeth me. My vision is spiritual, eternal, and a quality of my consciousness. My eyes are divine ideas, and they always function perfectly. My perception of spiritual truth is clear and powerful. The light of understanding dawns in me; I see more and more of God's truth every day. I see spiritually; I see mentally; I see physically. I see images of truth and beauty everywhere.

The infinite Healing Presence is now, this moment, rebuilding my eyes. They are perfect, divine instruments, enabling me to receive messages from the world within and the world without. The glory of God is revealed in my eyes.

I hear the truth; I love the truth; I know the truth. My ears are God's perfect ideas, functioning perfectly at all times. My ears are the perfect instruments that reveal God's harmony to me. The love, beauty, and harmony of God flow through my eyes and ears; I am in tune with the Infinite. I hear the still, small voice of God within me. The Holy Spirit quickens my hearing, and my ears are open and free.

STEP THIS WAY FOR A HEALING

1. People may say it's impossible, but with God all things are possible. You can be healed by God, who created you.

2. The healing principle flows through your mental patterns of thought and imagery, bringing all things you wish into manifestation.

3. If you believe something, it will be manifest— whether or not you are consciously thinking of it. Believe only in that which heals, blesses, and inspires you.

4. Exalt the power of God in the midst of you, and you will stop the spread of any disease in your body.

5. The thankful heart is close to God. Let all your prayers be made known with praise and thanksgiving.

6. You are spiritually blind when you don't know that thoughts are things, that what you feel you attract, and that what you imagine, you become.

7. Vision is spiritual, eternal, and indestructible. A wonderful prayer for the eyes is to affirm regularly: "I see better spiritually, mentally, and physically."

8. *I will lift up mine eyes unto the hills, from whence cometh my help* (Ps. 121:1).

LAW 4

THE DYNAMIC LAW OF PROTECTION

Some time ago, I was asked to visit a woman named Gloria W., who was being treated for cancer at the Sloan Kettering Institute in New York. When I asked about her family, she told me she had one son and two grandchildren, but she never saw them.

"Why is that?" I wondered. "Do they live far away?"

"No, they're an hour away, in Connecticut," she replied. "I never see them, because if I did I'd have to see my son's wife, too."

Puzzled, I asked, "Your daughter-in-law?"

"My son's wife," she repeated, deliberately rejecting the term I had suggested. Her face hardened. "I hate that little snip! I've hated her like poison since the accursed day my son brought her home. I can't imagine what he saw in her. I can only pray that his eyes are opened before it's too late."

"How long have your son and his wife been married?" I asked.

Gloria thought for a moment, then said, "Almost thirty years. And my feeling about her has grown stronger inside me every year!"

"Like your cancer," I remarked.

She stared at me. "What do you mean by that?" she demanded.

"Have you asked your doctors what caused your disease?" I replied. "If you strip away the technicalities, they probably said that some of your own cells have turned against you, have become poisonous. I'd like to suggest that in another sense the destructive emotions you've harbored toward your daughter-in-law have had a toxic effect on you. Not only on your mind and heart, but on the very cells of your body. Do you want to be cured of your cancer?"

"Of course I do!" she burst out. "More than anything!"

"More than your negative feelings about your daughter-in-law?" I probed. After a brief hesitation, she nodded. "Then you must give them up. You must teach yourself to practice the great art of forgiveness. You must begin by wholeheartedly, sincerely, and lovingly praying for your daughter-in-law."

Later in our encounter I helped Gloria compose this prayer about her daughter-in-law:

The peace of God fills her soul; she is inspired and blessed in all her ways. God is prospering her, and I rejoice that the law of God is working for her, through her, and all around her. I feel in my heart and soul that I have released her. Whenever the thought of her enters my mind, I wish her well. I am now free.

Gloria's spirit of forgiveness, together with the chemotherapy and other treatments she received, brought about a remarkable change in her personality, and a wonderful healing took place. Her prayer changed her subconscious mind by eliminating and neutralizing all the negative patterns lodged therein, and its embodiment also had to disappear.

A NEW CONCEPT OF GOD WORKS WONDERS

A few months ago, I was invited to visit a very kind man named Milton S. I knew him to be noble, generous, and magnanimous in every way. On my first evening as his guest, he told me that he had recently been diagnosed with prostate cancer.

"My father and uncle both died of prostate cancer," he added. "For twenty years or more, I've lived with the fear of developing it myself. I don't think a day has passed when I didn't pray to be spared this trial. Clearly my prayers did not find favor with God. It's just as Job said: 'The thing I greatly feared has come upon me.'"

"Old friend," I said, "forgive me, but I think your prayers have been misaddressed. What you have been doing is begging some far-off God, saying, 'If it is God's will, he will heal me. If not, he will inflict some dread disease on me.' This is nothing more than the primitive concept of an avenging God punishing his children. God dwells in each one of us. Because you believed yourself to be the likely victim of cancer by God's will, it was as if you willed it to happen. And so it did."

"If this is so," Milton asked, "what must I do to be saved?"

"Believe that your condition will be cured," I replied. "Be of good cheer. Approach the treatments your physician prescribes with the conviction that God wills them to be effective. Feel the cure in your heart, and your subconscious mind will respond accordingly."

Later I received word from Milton that his prostate cancer was in remission and his general health, both physical and spiritual, had never been better.

WHY SHE HAD NO BOYFRIENDS

Anne G. was a young woman from rural Wyoming who was working in an office in Los Angeles. She came to me after a public lecture and said, "Do you think you can help me? I'm so shy and timid that I blush and turn away if a fellow even says hello to me. I never learned how to get along with guys. I think maybe I never will."

"But you want to?" I probed.

"Oh, more than anything!" she exclaimed. "I hate being single and lonely. I want to make someone happy. I want a family of my own."

After we talked a bit longer, I explained to her how to realize her desires. The starting point was to abandon her view of herself as timid and withdrawn. She had to make herself feel that she was admired, wanted, and cared for.

At my suggestion, she bought a diary at a stationery store and started to fill it with accounts of dates with imaginary admirers. Every evening, she set aside a time to meditate on the details of these encounters, which were always positive and fulfilling. Soon she found that speaking to people at work was no longer so threatening to her. When a group of coworkers invited her to go along to a restaurant on a Friday evening, she accepted. One of them, a young man she had long admired from afar, spent the whole evening flirting and chatting with her. At the end of the evening, he asked to see her again. She soon became immensely popular with men and was no longer a wallflower.

As her romantic life began to flourish, Anne realized that she now wanted something more lasting. She began to affirm and claim that Infinite Intelligence was attracting to her an ideal companion who would harmonize with her perfectly. She imagined a wedding ring on her finger as she went to sleep at night. She would mentally "touch" and "feel" the ring. She actualized the state and impregnated her subconscious mind by feeling the naturalness, solidity, and tangibility of the ring. Moreover, she told herself the ring implied that the marriage was already consummated and that she was resting in the accomplished fact. She soon attracted a wonderful man. Today they blend harmoniously in every way.

HOW HE BECAME
A SUPERIOR STUDENT

"I'm terribly worried about my son Sam," David K. told me. "He's just eleven, but I'm afraid his future is very bleak. His teacher recently told me he thought Sam should be evaluated for a learning disability. There was talk of transferring him to a special education class. I know very well what that means. It's a polite way of saying he is retarded."

"What do you think?" I asked. "Could his teacher be correct?"

David shifted uncomfortably in his chair. "I hate to even think such a thing. But since that conference, I've been watching Sam very carefully. Sometimes he doesn't seem to hear what I say, and when I ask about his schoolwork, his responses come so slowly. It's as if it isn't penetrating his head."

"What line of work are you in, David?" I asked.

"I'm an advertising copywriter," he replied.

"Suppose the head of your department was secretly half convinced that you were a flop," I said. "Suppose he kept looking over your shoulder and asking you 'casual' questions about your assignments. What effect do you think that would have?"

"I'd fall flat on my face in no time," David said. "Oh— I see what you're getting at. The way I've been watching Sam is really sabotaging him. The same with his teacher. Anything that seems like a problem gets noticed more."

"That is a lot of it," I said. "But there's more. Your conscious belief that your son may be mentally disabled communicates itself to your subconscious *and to Sam's*. That helps bring about the very thing you fear."

"That's awful!" David said. "I don't want to harm Sam, I want to help him! But what can I do?"

"You must change your conscious beliefs," I told him. "Go someplace quiet, relax your body and mind, and lose yourself in the joy of hearing your boy tell you how well he's doing in school. Do this three or four times a day. Visualize him handing you a semester report with glowing comments from the teacher. Feel the solidity of the form in your hand, see the black letters on the white surface, hear yourself saying, 'Wow, Sam! Great work! Keep it up!'"

David adopted this advice. He immersed himself in this imagery until it penetrated his subconscious and became a living conviction. His son responded beautifully and blossomed forth as one of the best students in his class. The father experienced the fruit of the idea on which he had meditated. The father's prayer caused the intelligence and wisdom of the subconscious to well up in the mind of the boy, and he fulfilled his father's conviction of him.

HE COULD NOT BE SHOT

A few years ago I gave a series of lectures in Osaka, Japan. One evening in the restaurant of my hotel, I got into a conversation with a Japanese man named Akiro I. He told me he had served in the Imperial Army during World War II.

"This was in China," he said. "A fellow soldier who disliked me accused me of something I hadn't done. The court martial did not believe me. I was sentenced to be shot."

"How terrifying!" I said. "How did you escape the sentence?"

"I should tell you that as a boy I was sent to a Christian school," he replied. "In prison, some heavenly impulse made me keep repeating to myself the words of the Ninety-first Psalm. Then each night, before I went to sleep, I said to my profoundest self, 'I cannot be shot. I am God's child, and God cannot shoot himself.' I knew there is but one Power and one Life. My life was God's life."

Akiro told me that a few days before he was scheduled to be executed, he was released with no explanation and ordered back to duty. He never learned why he had been spared, but he was convinced that he had written his freedom in his subconscious mind by reiterating the truths of the Psalm and by picturing his freedom. Whatever you impregnate your subconscious with, it responds accordingly.

YOUR ANSWER DETERMINES YOUR FUTURE

When I was a boy at family gatherings, I used to hear my uncles and aunts talking about many things. Often, they would say, "You know, John or Mary met with that accident because he or she ceased going to church." Whenever any calamity came to people they knew, somehow they always found a reason to consider the victims sinful and the object of the wrath of God.

Even as a child, I often wondered what kind of a God they had in their minds. What is your concept of God? Do you know that the answer you give to that question inevitably determines your entire future?

YOUR BELIEF ABOUT GOD IS YOUR BELIEF ABOUT YOURSELF

If you think that God is cruel, vindictive, and an inscrutable, tyrannical, cannibalistic Moloch in the skies, a sort of despot whose goal is to punish you, of course, you will experience the result of this habitual thinking. Your life will be hazy, confused, and full of fear and limitations of all kinds. In other words, you will experience the results of the nature of your belief about God. You will actually have negative experiences because of your belief.

God becomes to you whatever you consider Him to be. Above all things, get the right concept of God. It makes no difference what you call God. You may call him Allah, Brahma, Vishnu, Reality, Infinite Intelligence, the Healing Presence, the Oversoul, Divine Mind, the Architect of the Universe, the Supreme Being, the Life Principle, the Living Spirit, or the Creative Power. The point is, your belief or conviction about God governs and gives direction to your whole life.

BELIEVE IN A GOD OF LOVE

Millions of people believe in a God who sends sickness, pain, and suffering; they believe in a cruel and vindictive Deity. They do not have a good God and, to them, God is not a loving God. Having such weird, ignorant concepts of God, they experience the results of their beliefs in the form of all kinds of difficulties and troubles. Your subconscious mind manifests your beliefs and projects them as experiences, conditions, and events.

Your nominal belief about God is meaningless. The thing that matters is your real, subconscious belief—the belief of your heart. You will always demonstrate your belief. That is why Dr. Quimby said, more than a century ago, "Man is belief expressed." Millions of people conceive of a God of caprice, far off in the skies, who possesses all the whims of a human being. With such a concept, they are like the business executive who once told me, "I would be all right if God would just leave me alone." Believe that God is love, that he watches over you and cares for you, and that he guides, prospers, and loves you. Wonders will happen in your life that will far exceed your fondest dreams!

BECOMING A NEW PERSON

His name shall be called Wonderful, Counsellor, The mighty God, The everlasting Father, The Prince of Peace (Is. 9:6).

Begin now, today, as you read these lines, to enthrone the true concept or belief about God, and miracles will begin to happen in your life. Realize and know that God is all bliss, joy, indescribable beauty, absolute harmony, infinite intelligence, and boundless love, and that He is omnipotent, supreme, and the only Presence.

Accept mentally that God is all these things, as unhesitatingly as you accept the fact that you are alive. Then you will begin to experience in your life the wonderful results of your new conviction about the blessed God within you. You will find your health, your vitality, your business, your environment, and the world in general changing for the better. You will begin to prosper spiritually, mentally, and materially. Your understanding and spiritual insight will grow in a wonderful way, and you will find yourself transformed into a new person.

HIS BUSINESS PROSPERED THREE-HUNDRED PERCENT

Philo L. came to speak to me after a lecture in London, England.

"I have lived with a deathly fear of poverty all my life," he admitted. "I work very hard, but my affairs do not flourish. What can I do?"

"Can you bring yourself to look upon God as your silent partner?" I asked. "As your guide and counselor? Believe that God always watches over you like a loving parent. Claim boldly that God is supplying all your needs and inspiring you in everything you do."

His face brightened. "How marvelous!" he said. "I never thought of God that way before. Always He was a distant, awesome Presence. But even a very stiff, dignified person unbends when he plays with his child. Perhaps it is the same with God!"

Philo wrote to me a few months later. "I feel God is a Living Presence, a friend, a counselor, and a guide," he said. "My business has prospered three-hundred percent, my health is better, and I have thrown away the thick lenses I wore for twenty years!"

You can see what happened when this man decided to look upon God as his Father. The word "father" meant something to him. It meant love, protection, guidance, and supply. Let wonders happen the same way in your life.

THE MIRACLE OF THREE STEPS

In the course of my ministry, I performed the marriage ceremony for a wonderful young couple, Janet and Bill S., in the Midwest. After about a month, however, they separated. Janet returned to her parents' home. What had happened to their romance?

When I asked Bill that question, he said, "We should never have stayed here, where we both grew up. Janet was just too popular. Practically every guy in our high school class was in love with her. Even before the wedding, I kept thinking she would start seeing other men. I was jealous of her. I did not trust her. I imagined that she was with some of her former boyfriends. I was sure I would lose her."

By imagining evil about his wife, Bill was cohabiting mentally with fear, jealousy, and loss. He had already broken his marriage vows. He had promised to cherish, love, and honor her at all times and, forsaking all others, to remain faithful to her alone. Instead, he embraced his own mistrust. His fear communicated itself to the subconscious mind of his wife. So it came to pass that what he feared and believed actually took place. Hurt and baffled by his attitude, Janet looked for sympathy and comfort with an old male friend, who still hoped to win her over. When Bill saw his belief made manifest, he blamed his wife. In truth, however, it was done unto him as he believed.

It was my pastoral duty to explain all this to Bill and Janet. Once they learned about the workings of their conscious and subconscious minds, they decided to pray together and to practice the miracle of three steps.

- **The first step: In the beginning, God.** The moment they awakened in the morning, they claimed God was guiding them in all their ways. They sent out loving thoughts of peace, harmony, and joy to each other and to the whole world.

- **The second step: Grace at meals.** They gave thanks for the wonderful food and for all of their blessings. They made sure that no problems, worries, or arguments entered into their table conversation.

- **The third step: Prayer before rest.** They kept
  their Bible close at hand and read a selection from
  it each night before going to sleep. These included
  the Twenty-third, Twenty-seventh, and Ninety-first
  Psalms, the eleventh chapter of Hebrews, and the
  thirteenth chapter of 1 Corinthians. They said quietly, "Thank you, Father, for all the blessings of the
  day. God giveth his beloved sleep."

Both Bill and Janet made a private vow to stop doing
the things that created distance from the other. This took
discipline plus an intense desire on both sides to make their
marriage work. As they followed this practical procedure,
harmony eventually was restored to them.

THE COUPLE WAS REUNITED

I had a rather strange interview a few years ago with Duane
R. and Margie B., who came to see me at my hotel in
Dallas, Texas. They were both worried and anxious.

"We used to be married," Duane told me. "To each other,
I mean. Then we broke up. I was a stupid, pigheaded mule,
or it wouldn't have happened."

"That's not fair," Margie protested. "I acted like an
idiot, and you know it!"

"Well, we won't fight over that now," Duane said. "The
point is, after going round and round, we got divorced.
Before long, we both got married again."

"You've heard about marrying on the rebound?"
Margie asked me. "Well, that's what it was. Talk about

making a mistake as big as all outdoors! The worst part is, I knew it before a week was out."

"Me too," Duane said. "Anyway, the point is, we tried to fight this thing for the last year and a half, and it's not working. We realize that we still love each other. What do we do?"

"Which do you think is more in accord with God's plan?" I asked. "A real marriage built on love, or a sham marriage built on lies?"

"A real marriage," they both said in the same breath.

"Then you have your answer," I said. "To live a lie with your present spouses is not just or fair to them or to yourselves. You must tell them the truth. I think you will find that, on some level, they know it already."

Duane and Margie were able to allow the inner love for one another in their hearts to lead them back to the altar of love. The "rebound" marriages were dissolved amicably, and all those involved were blessed thereby. The couple was reunited.

Love binds two hearts together, and it is an indissoluble link. *What therefore God* (Love) *hath joined together, let no man put asunder* (Matt. 19:6).

THE TRANSFORMING POWER OF LOVE

Elizabeth Y. came to me deeply distressed. "Do you believe that my father can use mental powers to destroy my marriage?" she asked.

"I'm not sure I understand the question," I replied. "Can you tell me more about the situation?"

She took a deep breath. "I've been married for almost a year and a half. Frank and I are deeply in love and very happy. The problem is, Frank is a Catholic, and my dad hates Catholics. He says they are enslaved to Satan. I know he is praying for my marriage to fall apart, and I am terrified that his prayers will work. Prayers *do* work, don't they? Isn't that what you teach?"

"Well, yes and no," I said. "Your prayers can work for you. But your father has no more power over you than a rabbit's foot or a pebble from a rocky shore . . . *unless you grant him that power.* If you listen and believe that he can destroy your marriage, his work is already half done. But if you use your own thoughts and feelings to strengthen your marriage, your father will be helpless to combat it."

At my suggestion, Elizabeth began to pray frequently that just as God's love had united her with her husband in the beginning, His love would continue to unite them now, surrounding them and enfolding them. She affirmed regularly that the beauty, love, and harmony of God permeated their minds and hearts and that God's love ruled their lives. She realized that nothing could come between her and the man she loved.

Love is of the heart. As this young husband and wife found love, grace, and good will in one another, and saw the virtues of each other, their marriage grew more blessed every day. The young woman prayed for divine understanding for her father, and she told me recently that he was becoming more tolerant now and was learning to love her husband.

PRAYER TRANSFORMED
A CRIMINAL

I once visited a man, Josh B., who was dying from the effects of chronic alcoholism. He told me that his drinking had led him to commit many crimes. "What do you think?" he asked. "Will God punish me? Am I on my way to hell?"

"God is a loving God," I replied. "He punishes no one. But we, by our misuse of the laws of life, punish ourselves, either through ignorance or by willfully violating the laws of harmony, love, and right action. You must forgive yourself and let God's love enter your soul. If you resolve to be a new man in God, then the past will be wiped out and remembered no more."

We prayed together. Afterward, Josh appeared radiant and happy. The reason for this was that he now had a deep inner faith and conviction that he was on the right side of God and that all was forgiven. He was very relaxed and said he was ready for what he called "heaven." His doctor noticed a remarkable improvement in the man, and soon thereafter he was told that he would live. Indeed, within ten days he left the hospital, whole and healthy again!

Josh is now eighty-five years old, still strong and healthy. He has become a wonderful, upright, God-like man—completely transformed. How did all this come about? It was the result of his acceptance of the truth about God. His complete surrender of all his crimes, hates, and guilt immediately released his mind and body. His body responded in a miraculous manner to his new mental attitude. His inner sense of freedom and peace of mind—nothing else—was the healing agent.

PRAYER SAVED HIS LIFE

I was visiting a friend in the hospital. As I got up to leave, he urged me to talk to the man in the next bed, Robert C. He told me in a whisper that Robert was on the critical list with a widespread systemic infection that did not respond to antibiotics. He was not expected to live.

I introduced myself to Robert. He seemed glad to have a distraction. As we talked about the hospital, he suddenly said, "The worst part of being here is that I know Harry is gloating like anything. I loathe that man. They don't come any lower than him."

"Who is he?" I asked.

"He was my partner," Robert told me. "Then I found out he was cooking the books and diverting the company's assets. I barely managed to avoid bankruptcy as a result. I tell you what, if I ever get out of this hospital bed, he'd better watch himself. I just might get around to giving him what he deserves!"

It was easy to see that Robert's loathing had become a festering psychic wound.

"Would you invite your former partner to dinner?" I asked.

"Only if I knew I could get away with poisoning him!" he declared.

"Yet you entertain him constantly in your mind," I pointed out, "and it is not he who is being poisoned. It is you. You give him—or rather, your psychic image of him—immense power over your mind, your body, and your vital organs. You are the only thinker in your universe. That means you are directly responsible for the thoughts, concepts, and images that come to you. If you saturate your mind with hatred and loathing, the effects will surely make themselves known in your body. But if you saturate your mind with the truths of God, only wholeness and health can follow."

Before leaving, I gave Robert a prayer to meditate on, which makes up the next section of this chapter. I later heard that he had made a rapid and unexpected recovery from his infection. Truly, wonders happen as you pray!

THE POWER OF GOD

This prayer has helped many people to transform their lives. As you meditate on these wonderful truths, you too will shortly discover that wonders are happening in your life!

God is the only Presence and the only Power, and I am one with it. God's strength is my strength; His Intelligence floods my mind. This new awareness gives me complete dominion in every department of my life. I am now joined to the One Universal Mind, which is God. His wisdom, power, and glory flow through me. I know that the energy and power of God permeate every atom, tissue, muscle, and bone of my being, making me perfect now. God is Life, and this Life is my life. My faith is renewed; my vitality is restored. God walks and talks in me. He is my God; I am one with Him. His truth is my shield and buckler; I rejoice that it is so. Under His wings shall I trust. I dwell in the Secret Place of the Most High, and I abide under the Shadow of the Almighty.

POINTS TO REMEMBER

1. Hatred is a mental poison. Forgiveness and love are the spiritual antidotes to use, and then a healing follows.

2. Get a new concept of God as Love. Realize that God is *for* you, not against you.

3. Your mental attitude is cause, and your experience is effect.

4. You can protect yourself from all harm by realizing that God's love surrounds you, enfolds you, and enwraps you.

5. Believe in your heart the truths expounded in the Ninety-first Psalm, and you will be invulnerable.

6. Imagine and feel that you are loved, wanted, and appreciated, and you will never lack friends.

7. Pray for the so-called special child by calling forth in prayer and meditation the intelligence and wisdom of God, which are inherent in all children.

8. Mentally write your freedom in your subconscious mind, and it will respond accordingly.

9. Your real belief about God determines your whole fate.

10. Your belief about God is your real belief about yourself. "Man is belief expressed" (Quimby*).

11. Your nominal belief about God is meaningless. What really matters is the belief in your heart.

12. Believe that God is all bliss, peace, beauty, joy, and love, and that what is true of God is true of you. Make a habit of this, and wonders will happen in your life!

13. Boldly claim that God supplies all your needs, and you will prosper in all your ways.

14. Your habitual fears can be communicated to the subconscious of your spouse. Form a habit of thinking on that which is lovely and of good report.

15. When God's love unites a husband and wife, no person, place, or condition can break up the marriage. Love is the indissoluble link that binds.

16. God, or Life, punishes no one. We punish our-
    selves, either through ignorance or by willfully
    violating the laws of harmony, love, and right
    action.

17. Hatred is a deadly poison, causing the death of all
    the vital organs of the body.

*From *The Complete Writings of Phineas Parkhurst
Quimby*, De Vorso & Co., 1988.

Law 5

The Mysterious Law of Inner Guidance

Like all of us, you are sometimes perplexed, confused, and fearful. You wonder what decision to make. When that happens to you, remember that you have an inner guide that will lead and direct you in all your ways. It can reveal to you the perfect plan and show you the way you should go. The secret of guidance or right action is to mentally devote yourself to the right answer until you find its response welling up within you.

The infinite intelligence deep in your subconscious mind is responsive to your request. You will recognize this response as an inner feeling, an awareness, an overpowering hunch leading you to the right place at the right time, putting the right words into your mouth, and causing you to do the right thing in the right way.

FOLLOW THE LEAD THAT COMES

A minister friend of mine, Mark A., once asked me if I thought the governing board of his church should buy the property of another church that was just falling vacant. I answered, "Let's pray about it and follow the lead that comes."

Nothing happened for the next few days. Then, one morning, Mark telephoned me.

"We're having a board meeting today," he said. "We have to decide. Do we buy the property or not?"

As he spoke, I felt an answer growing in my mind. It was "No." But I did not want to sway Mark's decision, so I said, "What do you think? Or rather, what do you feel?"

"It looks like a sensible, prudent course," he said, with hesitation in his voice. "But what do I feel? I feel it's the wrong decision."

"So do I," I told him.

The governing board argued but ultimately accepted Mark's recommendation. A couple of months later, it was discovered that the site they had decided not to buy was seriously contaminated by seepage from the underground tanks of a nearby service station.

THERE ALWAYS IS AN ANSWER

Greta P., a listener to my radio program, wrote to me. She wrote, in part:

I live in a four-family house, which I own. I depend on the income to supplement my pension. One of my tenants was boisterous, rude, and noisy. He often had drunken parties in his apartment. To make matters worse, he was also behind in his rent, making it hard for me to pay *my* bills on time. My other tenants are quiet, older people who were very bothered by his behavior. I asked him to leave, but he refused with curses. Then my best tenants told me they were looking for a new place to live. I was at my wits' end!

One day after listening to your program, I realized that the answer was within me. I quieted my mind and prayed that the infinite intelligence in the subconscious mind of my unruly tenant would guide and direct him to his true place and would prompt him to leave in peace and harmony at once. I affirmed, "I release him completely. I loose him and let him go, wishing for him peace, love, and happiness."

As I prayed in this way, I came to a point where my mind was filled with inner peace and tranquillity. I knew that meant my prayer would be answered, and so it was. That same evening, the tenant came to my door, paid every penny he owed me, and announced that he was moving someplace a little livelier. Three days later, after I posted a notice at the local supermarket, an intelligent, soft-spoken older man came to look at the vacant apartment. He took it on the spot. It turns out he is a listener of yours as well. My prayer was answered in every way!

A BUSINESSWOMAN'S GUIDANCE FORMULA

At a dinner to benefit a local charity, I found myself at the same table with Adrienne W., who runs a successful media relations firm. As we chatted, the question of decision making came up.

"I have a very simple technique," Adrienne said. "You may think it is *too* simple, but it works very well for me."

Intrigued, I asked, "What is it? Will you share it with us?"

"I'd be delighted," she replied. "Whenever an important question comes up that calls for a quick decision—and that seems to be at least once every day—I go into my office, shut the door, turn off the phone, and meditate on the divine qualities I believe are within me and everyone. I find myself being transported into a mood of peace, power, and confidence."

A man sitting across the table, who was listening, interjected, "I'd give a lot to get some of that into *my* daily life!"

"I'm sure you can, if you try," Adrienne said. "Once I find myself in that place, I say, 'Father, thou knowest all things. Give me the idea I need for this new program,' or this problem, or whatever it is. Then I visualize having the answer, feeling it flow through my mind, complete and perfect. At that point I think, 'I accept the answer and I give thanks for it.'"

The woman sitting on the other side of her, a commodities broker, said, "But you don't really have it, do you? You're just saying that."

Adrienne smiled. "My grandmother used to say, 'Well begun is half done.' Once I finish my prayer, I get busy with other matters. I put the matter out of my mind. I've found that the answer usually comes when I least expect it. It's like a flash of light in a dark room, that suddenly reveals everything at once. I have to say this, too: I imagine I've made as many faulty business decisions as anyone. But not once have I been disappointed by the answers that come when I follow this procedure. Not once!"

A PROFESSOR GETS
A SPECIFIC ANSWER

Alan F. is a professor at a local university who attends my public lectures. After one such lecture, we started talking. I remarked that he seemed perturbed. Was there something wrong?

"Indeed there is," he said. "I am currently drafting a paper about archaeological excavations in Egypt during the nineteenth century. I am very nearly finished, but there is one section I cannot verify. The only reliable source for the information is a book that was privately published in a limited edition in Cairo in 1884. I've used the internet to check the catalogues of all the major libraries of the world. So far, I have not managed to locate a copy of the book in any of them. Yet without it, I do not feel confident that I can submit my article for publication."

"You're in a difficult position," I said sympathetically. "May I make a suggestion?"

"Please do," he said, suddenly alert.

"Here is what I would do in a situation like yours," I continued. "Tonight, before going to bed, I would put myself into a calm, relaxed frame of mind. As I was going to sleep, I would say to myself, silently and with total confidence, 'My subconscious knows the answer, and it gives me all the information I need.' Then I would drop off to sleep with the one word, 'answer,' in my mind."

"And you believe this would be helpful?" he asked.

"Yes, I do," I replied. "Your subconscious mind is all-wise. It knows what type of answer you need. It will answer in a dream, as an overpowering hunch, or as a feeling that you are being led on the right track. You may get a sudden flash of intuition to go to a certain place, or another person may give you the answer."

Later that week, Alan called me. "It's unbelievable!" he exclaimed. "I used the technique you told me about for three nights. Then, yesterday morning, as I arrived on campus, something drew me to one of the bulletin boards. Ordinarily, I walk right past them, but I couldn't. I scanned the notices, and my eye was pulled toward one announcing a used book sale to benefit a campus organization that promotes New Age ideas. It was to take place that same day at noon, on the other side of campus."

"And you went?" I asked.

"Indeed I did," he replied. "When I walked in, I wondered what I was doing there. Tables full of trashy best-selling paperbacks, volumes of condensed books, outdated software manuals, guides to building a barbecue pit . . . you know the sort of thing you find at these affairs. But at that moment, a man arrived carrying a carton of books. I heard him tell the student in charge that his late uncle was into mystical stuff like the Pyramids, and these were some of his old books."

"I think I see where you are going," I said.

"Perhaps you do," he said. "I asked if I might look through the books, since that was a field that interested me. I opened the carton, and the second book that came to hand was precisely the rare volume I had given up hope of finding! Incidentally, several other books were of great interest, too. I gave the organization a check for twice the amount they wanted to charge for the books."

ALWAYS BE ON THE ALERT

Sometimes, divine guidance comes to us in the form of a fleeting impression. We must always be on the alert for them. When a feeling or idea comes to us, we must recognize it and follow it.

BE STILL AND RELAXED

There are two reasons why we may not acknowledge our inner guidance. These are tension and failure to recognize the lead when it comes. If we are in a happy, confident, joyous mood, we will recognize the flashes of intuition that come to us. Moreover, we will feel under a subjective compulsion to carry them out.

Therefore, it is necessary to be still and relaxed when you pray for guidance. Nothing can be achieved by tenseness, fear, or apprehension. Your subconscious mind answers you when your conscious mind is still, receptive, and relaxed.

SHE GETS WONDERFUL SLOGANS

Dora P. is celebrated in our local advertising community for her wonderful slogans. This is how she creates them: She drops off to sleep with the words "right slogan" on her lips. She is confident that the answer will be forthcoming—and it always is. *He faileth not* (Zeph. 3:5).

INTUITION PAYS FABULOUS DIVIDENDS

The word intuition means *taught from within*. Intuition goes much further than reason. You employ reason to carry out intuition. Intuition is the spontaneous answer that wells up from your subconscious mind in response to your conscious thinking.

For business and professional people, the cultivation of the intuitive faculty is of great importance. Intuition offers instantaneously that which our intellect or reasoning mind could accomplish only after weeks or months of monumental trial and error.

When our reasoning faculties fail us in our perplexities, the intuitive faculty sings the silent song of triumph. The conscious mind is reasoning, analytical, and inquisitive;

the subjective faculty of intuition is always spontaneous. It comes as a beacon to the conscious intellect. Many times it speaks as a warning against a proposed trip or plan of action.

HOW A NOVELIST GETS MARVELOUS IDEAS

I once chatted with Siri N., a wonderful novelist in Calcutta. She told me that the secret of her success in writing is that she regularly and systematically claims that God is guiding her in all her ways and that she will astonish the world with the beauties, glories, and gems of wisdom given to her by God within her.

Her favorite prayer is: "God knows all things. God is my Higher Self, the Spirit in me. God is writing a novel through me. He is giving me the theme, the characters and their names, and the locations and setting. He reveals the ideal drama in perfect sequence. I give thanks for the answer which I know is coming, and I go off to sleep with the word 'novel' on my lips, until I am lost in the deep of sleep."

Siri knows that the word *novel* will be etched on her subconscious mind and that the latter will respond. She said that usually, after praying this way prior to writing a novel, a few days later she would get the inner urge to write, and the words and scenes would flow in an unending stream.

This is representative of the miracle of divine guidance that is available to us all.

HE FOUND HIS TRUE PLACE

Nathan G. was a sales rep with a paper goods wholesaler. When he came to consult me, he said, "I'm a square peg in a round hole! I'm good at my job, but it's wearing me to a frazzle. I'm starting to *hate* paper goods! What can I do? Isn't there any place that's right for me?"

"Of course there is," I assured him. "There is an answer to your problem. The infinite intelligence and wisdom of your subconscious mind knows your talents and interests. It knows how to open the door for their perfect expression in life."

I directed him to pray as follows:

I believe and accept without question that there is a creative intelligence in my subconscious mind that knows all and sees all. I know that I am directed rightly to my true place in life. I accept this inner guidance without question. I am here for a purpose, and I am willing to fulfill that purpose now.

Nathan left my office in a very happy mood. Two weeks later, he telephoned. "I prayed, the way we said I should," he told me, "and I kept finding myself thinking about gourmet foods. I've always been interested in them, but mostly as a customer. I started wondering. You know, a lot of the accounts I serviced in my job are stores that carry lines of fancy foods. What if this was my real interest? So I called up and made an appointment with the head of the best gourmet wholesaler in the area. When I went in, something made me say just the right words. To make a long story short, I got the job, and I already know it's what I always wanted."

A PRAYER FOR DIVINE GUIDANCE

I know that there is a perfect law of supply and demand. My motives are right, and I desire to do the right thing in the right way at all times. I am instantly in touch with everything I need. I am in my true place now; I am giving of my talents in a wonderful way, and I am divinely blessed. Infinite Intelligence is guiding me now in thought, word, and deed, and whatever I do is controlled by God and by God alone. I am a perfect channel of God.

I feel, know, and believe that my God-Self illumines my pathway. Divine Intelligence inspires, directs, and governs me in all my undertakings and instantaneously reveals to me the answer to all things I need to know. Divine love goes before me, making all roads a highway of peace, love, joy, and happiness. It is wonderful!

IDEAS TO REMEMBER

1. Mentally and emotionally devote yourself to the right answer, and you will get a response.

2. Infinite Intelligence in your subconscious mind knows all and sees all. Call upon it and you will receive an answer. It knows only the answer.

3. Follow the lead that comes. Often, it flashes spontaneously into your conscious mind.

4. Remember that there is always an answer. Persevere and relax, and you will find wonders happening when you pray.

5. Praying for guidance is a two-way conversation. Ask your deeper mind for the answer with faith and confidence, and you will receive an answer.

6. Your subconscious mind answers you in unknown ways. You may be led to a bookstore and pick up a book that answers your question, or you may overhear a conversation that provides the solution to your problem. The answers may come in countless ways.

7. It is necessary to be alert and alive, so that you will recognize the lead that comes, and then follow it.

8. The wisdom of your subconscious rises to your surface mind, or conscious mind, when the latter is relaxed and at peace. Relaxation is the key.

9. Drop off to sleep with the word "answer" on your lips, repeating it over and over again as a lullaby, and the appropriate answer will be given to you.

10. You use your intellect to carry out the voice of intuition.

11. If you are a novelist or a writer, claim that the wis-

dom of your subconscious is revealing to you the theme and characters, prompting you in all ways. You will be amazed at the results.

12. Infinite Intelligence within you will guide you to your true place and reveal your hidden talents.

13. Affirm, "Divine love goes before me, making straight, joyous, glorious, and happy my ways." All your ways will be ways of pleasantness and all your paths will be paths of peace.

LAW 6

THE MIGHTY LAW OF COURAGE

Fear is a powerful force, but you can learn to live so that fear will no longer dominate you. Your fear may reach back into the past, perhaps even into the inheritance of the collective mind, but you need not stay subject to it. While there are many primitive fears in the subconscious of all of us, you can eradicate all those fears by joining mentally and emotionally with the God-Presence within you. As you learn to love God and all things good, and as you trust Him implicitly, you will overcome your fears and become a free and fearless person.

HOW PRAYER FREED HER FROM PANIC

A few years ago, a young woman named Marie P., whom I did not know, phoned me at the Algonquin Hotel in New York City.

"My father always talked about your ideas," she said. "He died recently. I know he hid a large sum of money somewhere in the house. I'm really desperate. If I don't find the money, I might end up losing the house!"

"Have you tried to ask your subconscious mind?" I asked.

"No, I've never done anything like that," she replied. "I wouldn't know how to begin."

"Well, I will pray for a solution to your problem," I told her. "Will you come to see me tomorrow?"

That same night, I had a dream in which a man I didn't know said, "Get up and write this down. You are seeing my daughter Marie tomorrow."

Still half asleep, I got up, went to the desk, and found a sheet of hotel stationery. The figure in my mind dictated to me as I wrote. I am sure that these instructions were not written by Joseph Murphy, or even by my subconscious in the half-dreamworld where I then was.

I am firmly persuaded that the author was the father of the girl whom I was to see the following day. His personality, which had survived what we call death, gave me detailed instructions for locating a large sum of money that was hidden in his home. It also gave details of holdings in the Bahamas, with explicit instructions to his daughter on whom to contact to take possession of them.

The next day, Marie visited me at the Church of Religious Science headquarters in New York City. I recognized her immediately, because I had seen her in my dream the night before. There is a shining facet of our subconscious mind that reflects what is subjectively perceived and known, but not consciously known.

The acute anxiety Marie suffered was needless. All the time her subconscious knew where the money was. If she had known how, she could have communicated with it and received her answer. Since then, the study of the laws of her mind has completely transformed her life. Today she is vital and alive and accomplishing great things.

HER PRAYER CAST OUT HER FEAR

Amanda C. is a talented musician who relocated to New York City and opened a music studio. She advertised extensively; weeks passed and not one student appeared on the scene. She told me this after one of my lectures. "I'm so afraid," she confessed. "If I have to go back to Iowa as a total failure, I don't know what I'll do. I suppose I was a fool to try this. Of course I'm failing. Why should students come to me? They've never even heard of me!"

I pointed out to Amanda that her difficulties reflected her underlying attitude. She was convinced she would fail. She was positive that students would not come to her because she was unknown. Her basic trouble was her fear.

"If you can reverse your mental attitude, wonders may follow," I told her. "Do you believe that students will benefit by what you can teach them?"

"Oh, yes, I'm *sure* of it!" she proclaimed.

"Then you must build on that knowledge." I suggested a technique for her to use.

Twice daily Amanda imagined herself teaching her students and saw them happy and pleased with their progress. She was the star in the drama, "Act as though I am, and I will be." She felt herself to be the successful teacher, acting the role in her imagination, and focusing her attention on her ideal. Through her persistence, she became one with the idea in her mind until she succeeded in objectively manifesting what she subjectively imagined and felt. She attracted more students than she could handle and eventually had to take on an assistant.

What she imagined her life to be, she felt it to be, and according to her new feeling or mental attitude was it done unto her.

A GARDEN GAVE HIM COURAGE

While I was giving a series of lectures in Cape Town, South Africa, I made the acquaintance of Jonathan S., a retired colonel in the British army. He told me a little about his life as a prisoner of war during the Korean War. He spent eighteen months in solitary confinement, but he did not have a bitter word to say about his Chinese captors. In his imagination he walked around his garden in England and listened to the bells of his parish church welcoming him home. Colonel S. said, "The mental picture of this glorious place forever kept my mind alive. Not for one moment did I let it slip away."

Instead of resenting and hating, or indulging in mental recriminations, Colonel S. gave himself a constructive vision. He imagined himself home with his loved ones; he felt the thrill and joy of it all. Visualizing the garden in full bloom, he saw the plants grow and bring forth magnificent flowers. It was vivid and real in his mind. He felt all this inwardly in his imagination. He said other men might have gone insane or perhaps died of a broken heart, but he saved himself because he had a vision. "It was a vision I never let slip away."

Colonel S.'s great secret was a new mental attitude in the midst of privation, misery, and squalor. He was loyal to his mental picture, and he never deviated from it by destructive inner talking or negative mental imagery. When he finally arrived home in England, he realized the significance of the profound truth that we go where our vision is.

HE CAST OUT HIS UNKNOWN FEARS

Following a series of lectures I gave for the Science of Mind organization in San Francisco, a man named George B. visited me at my hotel. The first thing he said was, "I am haunted by unknown fears. I wake up at night sweating and shaking all over." He also suffered from hypertension and from frequent acute paroxysmal attacks of asthma.

As we talked, I eventually learned that George hated his late father. The reason was that the father had disapproved of George's lifestyle and as a result had bequeathed his entire, rather large, estate to George's sister. This hatred created a deep sense of guilt in his subconscious mind.

Because of this guilt, he had a deep, hidden fear of being punished. This complex expressed itself in his body as high blood pressure and asthmatic attacks.

Fear causes pain. Love and good will bring peace and health. The fear and guilt that George experienced manifested as disease.

As we talked, George came to see that his trouble was caused by his own sense of guilt, self-condemnation, and hatred. His father had long since passed to a higher dimension of life, but his memory was causing George to poison himself through hatred.

I was able to help George find the means to forgive his father and, as a result, forgive himself. He affirmed as follows:

> I completely forgive my father. He did what he believed right according to his light. I release him. I wish him peace, harmony, and joy. I am at peace with his memory and with myself.

Once George came to terms with his feelings, his asthma abated and his blood pressure dropped to normal. The fear of punishment that had been lurking in his subconscious mind has now disappeared.

SHE CEASED BLOCKING THE ANSWER

Joanna W. wrote to me in deep distress. "I don't know what to do or where to turn. I am overwhelmed with fear of doing the wrong thing. Should I take a new job I've been offered, or stay where I am? Should I keep or sell my home? Should I marry the man I've been dating? Where can I turn for answers? How can I decide what to do?"

I wrote back that it was her fear of doing the wrong thing that was blocking the answers Joanna so longed for. Furthermore, her fear was really based on a failure to understand the workings of her subconscious mind.

I explained that whenever her subconscious accepts an idea, immediately it begins to execute it. It uses all its mighty resources to that end. It mobilizes all the unlimited mental and spiritual powers in our depths. This law is true for good ideas, but also for bad ideas.

"Whenever you make such statements as 'I will never get an answer; I don't know what to do; I'm all mixed up,'" I wrote, "you block your access to the answers in your subconscious. If you express a clear confidence in the wisdom of the answer to come, then Infinite Intelligence within your subconscious will provide the answer."

Joanna took my advice. She prayed frequently as follows:

Infinite Intelligence is all-wise. The wisdom of my subconscious mind reveals to me the right answers. I am divinely guided regarding my home and my selection of a husband, and I am confident Infinite Intelligence knows my hidden talents and guides me to my true place in life where I am doing what I love to do, divinely happy and divinely prospered.

Joanna was inspired to leave her job for a new position with a major law firm. She later married her longtime beau and they both now live in her home. There was a perfect solution and an ideal answer to all her requests. The wisdom of the subconscious is past finding out.

WISE THOUGHTS

If your thought is wise, the reaction or response will be wise. Your action is only the outer expression of your thought. Your constructive action or decision is but the manifestation of a wise or true thought entertained in your mind.

After asking for guidance or an answer to a particular problem, do not neglect obvious or convenient stepping-stones to your goal. You will avoid blocking your answer when you simply think about the solution, knowing that your thought activates your subconscious, which knows all, sees all, and has what is needed to accomplish your goal.

CHOOSE CONFIDENCE, TRIUMPH, AND VICTORY

The Bible says *Choose you this day whom ye will serve* (Josh. 24:15). The key to health, happiness, peace of mind, and abundance lies in the capacity to choose. When you learn to think right, you will cease choosing pain, misery, poverty, and limitation. On the contrary, you will choose from the treasure-house of the Infinite within you. You will affirm incisively and decisively, "I choose happiness, peace, prosperity, wisdom, and security."

The moment you come to that definite conclusion in your conscious mind, your subconscious mind—full of the power and wisdom of the Infinite—will come to your aid. Guidance will come to you, and the way or path of achievement will be revealed to you.

Claim definitely and positively, without the slightest hesitation, doubt, or fear, "There is only one power of creation, and it is the power of my Deeper Self. There is a solution to every problem. This I know, decree, and believe." As you claim these truths boldly, you will receive guidance pertinent to all your undertakings, and wonders will happen in your life.

HOW SHE OVERCAME THE FEELING OF FRUSTRATION

Amelia H., a young automotive designer, came to me in frustration. "Every job I've ever had," she said, "my superior has had it in for me. I know I'm good at what I do, but my talents are being wasted. I think it must be because I'm a woman in what is still mostly a man's field. I got that all my life, starting with my father. He was so convinced that girls should grow up to get married, have lots of babies, and keep house. He still is, as far as I know. I've had no contact with him in three or four years."

"Why is that?" I asked. "Did he break off contact, or did you?"

"I was just so tired of his sermons!" she exclaimed. "I got to the point of hating to hear his voice. I know I should be more tolerant and understanding. He probably thinks his way is best for me. But I can't stand that old stuff. I won't put up with it. I don't care if he's my father, and I don't even care if God has it in for me because I hate my father!"

"Let me see if I understand what you're saying," I said. "You resent your father because of his outdated ideas about women. By choosing your career, you did more than resent his ideas, you actively rebelled against them. Is that right?"

"Well, of course," Amelia replied. "Wouldn't you, in my place?"

"Maybe so," I said. "But it occurs to me that you have been seeing your father in everyone who seems to have authority over you. That even includes God. Isn't it possible that you have been shifting the blame for your own short-comings and mistakes to your bosses, in order to justify a rebellious attitude that doesn't even have anything to do with them?"

Amelia overcame her sense of frustration by first per-ceiving that she was actually blocking her own progress by her fear, resentment, and hatred. She decided to pray morn-ing and evening as follows:

> I wish for everyone in the organization where I work health, happiness, peace, and promotion. My employer congratulates me on my work; I paint this picture in my mind regularly, and I know it will come to pass. I am loving, kind, and coop-erative. I practice the Golden Rule, and I sincerely treat everyone in the same way that I would like to be treated.

Divine Intelligence rules and guides me all day long, and I am prospered in all my ways.

As she saturated her mind regularly and systematically with these thoughts, Amelia succeeded in bringing about a new mental attitude that changed everything for the better in her life.

FIVE POSITIONS IN FIVE MONTHS

The young man who showed up in my office was, frankly, a mess. His name was Bernhart O., and he began by saying, "I got fired yesterday. That makes five jobs in five months. Do you think that's a record?" He went on to tell me he suffered from insomnia, alcoholism, and depression. What I found puzzling was that he seemed almost proud of this recital of problems.

"Why do you think you are fired so often?" I asked.

"They don't like me," he replied. "My bosses, the other people . . . none of them like me. Maybe it's my face, or something chemical."

"Are you a good worker?" I probed. "Do you show up every day on time and put a real effort into your job?"

He looked away. "It's not my fault," he mumbled. "Sometimes I just don't feel up to going. If I've been up all night, not able to sleep—"

"Or suffering from a terrible hangover?" I suggested.

"Yeah, that, too," he said. "Anyway, what's the use? They're not going to like me whatever I do, and sooner or later I'll get fired."

I explained to Bernhart that his dominant attitude of fear colored everything. His pessimistic, helpless outlook caused him to look at life from the dark or negative side. This led him to act lazy and shiftless. Of course his bosses didn't care for him and didn't keep him. Why should they? He gave them nothing and could expect nothing in return.

At my suggestion, Bernhart took a course in business fundamentals and another course in public speaking. With diligence, personal initiative, and application, he learned the rudiments of the commercial world. He began to pray for guidance and prosperity, claiming regularly that God was guiding him in all his ways and that he was prospered beyond his fondest dreams.

Gradually Bernhart's underlying attitude changed. He developed enthusiasm, perseverance, and a cooperative team spirit. He became happy and joyous and began to express health, harmony, and true living. On his next job, he was kept on after a probation period and soon was promoted to greater responsibilities.

Bernhart learned that practically all teaching, whether institutional, religious, or secular, has for its real purpose the inducement of a changed mental attitude toward life, people, and events. The first step in banishing his abnormal fear and in his onward march was correcting his attitude toward life.

HOW TO REALIZE YOUR DESIRE

No one can serve two masters. You cannot expect to realize the desire of your heart if you believe there is a power that thwarts that desire. This creates a conflict, and your mind is divided. You stand still and get nowhere. Your mind must move as a unity. Infinity cannot be divided or multiplied. The Infinite must be one—a unity. There cannot be two Infinities, as one would quarrel with the other; they would neutralize or cancel out each other. We would have chaos instead of a cosmos. Unity of the spirit is a mathematical necessity, for there is no opposition to the one Power. If there were some power to challenge God, or the Infinite One, God would cease to be omnipotent or supreme.

You can see what confusion and chaos reign in the minds of people who believe in two opposing powers. Their minds are divided because they have two masters, and this belief creates a conflict, causing their power and strength to be divided. Learn to go in one direction only, by believing that God who gave you the desire will also show you how to fulfill it.

TAKE A PERSONAL INVENTORY

Are you experiencing friction, misunderstanding, and resentment in your relationships with others? These unsatisfactory personal adjustments are due to the bad company you are keeping in your mind. When you were young, your parents warned you to keep away from bad company. If you disobeyed, you felt their disapproval. In a somewhat similar manner, you must not walk down the dark alleys of your mind and keep the company of resentment, fear, worry, ill will, and hostility. These are the thieves of your mind. They rob you of poise, balance, harmony, and health.

You must positively and definitely refuse to walk and talk with the negative feelings in the galleries of your mind. On the contrary, you must make it a practice to walk the sunlit streets of your mind, associating with lovely, spiritual companions called confidence, peace, faith, love, joy, good will, health, happiness, guidance, inspiration, and abundance. You can choose your companions in the objective world, and I feel sure that when you do you will select them according to the criteria of honesty and integrity.

You select your clothes, work, friends, teachers, books, home, and food. You are a choosing, volitional being. When you choose something, you enact a preference for one thing over another, even if it's only a hat or a pair of shoes. Having taken a personal inventory of the contents of your mind, choose health, happiness, peace, and abundance, and you will reap fabulous dividends.

UNDERSTANDING BANISHES NEEDLESS SUFFERING

You must give up your false beliefs, opinions, and theories. Exchange them for the truth that sets you free. You are not a victim of your five senses; neither are you controlled by external conditions or environment. You can change conditions by changing your mental attitude. Your thought and feeling create your destiny and determine your experience.

Therefore, you can no longer blame others for your misery, pain, or failure.

What you think, feel, believe, and give mental consent to, consciously or unconsciously, determines the happenings, events, and circumstances of your life. Once you thoroughly grasp that truth, you will cease to fear, resent, condemn, and blame others. You will discover there is no one to change but yourself.

YOU CREATE YOUR OWN HEAVEN

For countless centuries, people have looked outside themselves and filled their minds with jealousy, hate, fear, resentment, and depression, because they believed others were marring their happiness and causing their troubles. People have believed that they are the victims of fate, chance, and accidents, and that there are other powers and forces inimical to their welfare. Their minds are full of all sorts of weird ideas, superstitions, anxieties, and complicated philosophies about devils, evil entities, and malevolent forces.

The truth is that a person's thought is creative. Our habitual thinking becomes our abundance or our poverty. We must divest ourselves of all our erroneous and false concepts and realize that we make our own heaven (harmony and peace) and our own hell (misery and suffering), here and now.

You can influence your subconscious positively or negatively. The subconscious mind is always amoral and impersonal. It has no ethics or sentiments. Hence, if a person's thoughts are of an evil nature, the law of the subconscious mind will automatically bring these thoughts into form and experience. If someone's thoughts are good, wholesome, and constructive, the law of the subconscious will bring forth good experiences and happy circumstances.

This is neither more nor less than the law of cause and effect, which is a universal and impersonal law.

RETRIBUTION AND REWARD

Your retribution and reward depend on how you use your mind. If you make an erroneous decision in your mind, you invoke the mathematical and just response of the law of your subconscious mind. You will experience loss as a result of your erroneous judgment or decision. The law of action and reaction is universal throughout nature. If your thoughts are wise, your actions will be wise.

God is not vengeful or vindictive, but the impersonal law of your own mind reacts and responds according to what is impressed upon it. Your thought-life produces what seems like vengeance when you are unawakened to the way your mind works. Actually, you are experiencing a natural law of action and reaction, which is always equal, exact, and precise. Suppose a friend falls in a lake and drowns because he does not know how to swim. Would you blame the lake? Would you accuse it of acting vengefully? Of course not. The water is completely impersonal.

It simply obeys a physical law.

> I sent my soul through the Invisible
> Some letter of that after-life to spell,
> And by and by my soul returned to me
> And answered, "I myself am Heaven and Hell."
>   (*The Rubáiyát* by Omar Khayyam)

THE SECRET PLACE

I suggest you quiet the wheels of your mind frequently and dwell on these great eternal truths that live in the hearts of all people. *He that dwelleth in the secret place of the most High shall abide under the shadow of the Almighty* (Ps. 91:1). As you affirm the following prayer regularly, systematically, and joyously, you will feel rejuvenated, revitalized, and energized spiritually, mentally, and physically:

> I dwell in the secret place of the most High; this is my own mind. All the thoughts entertained by me conform to harmony, peace, and good will. My mind is the dwelling place of happiness, joy, and a deep sense of security. All the thoughts that enter my mind contribute to my joy, peace, and general welfare. I live, move, and have my being in the atmosphere of good fellowship, love, and unity.
>
> All the people who dwell in my mind are God's children. I am at peace in my mind with all the members of my household and all humankind. The same good I wish for myself, I wish for all people. I am living in the house of God now. I

claim peace and happiness, for I know I dwell in the house of the Lord forever.

IMPORTANT POINTERS

1. Eradicate fear by joining mentally and emotionally with the God-Presence within you.

2. If you can't find something, ask your subconscious and it will reveal the answer to you.

3. Many times hatred is the cause of fear of being punished. Forgive the other and go free.

4. Fear of failure will attract failure. Expect success, and good fortune will smile on you.

5. If confined or restricted, get a mental vision and mentally adhere to it. Be loyal to it, and you will go where your vision is.

6. Fear is behind many physical ailments. Fill your mind with love and good will, and you will be free.

7. Never say "I am full of fear" or "I am all mixed up." Your subconscious takes these statements literally, and you remain confused.

8. If your thoughts are wise, your actions will be wise.

9. The key to health, happiness, and peace of mind lies in the capacity to choose the abundant life.

10. You don't have to be frustrated. Realize that God who gave you the desire will bring it to pass in divine order. There is no power to oppose Omnipotence.

11. A changed attitude changes everything. Become enthusiastic, believe in yourself and in your hidden powers, and wonders will happen in your life.

12. The double-minded person is unstable in all ways. Be single-minded. Recognize the One Power, and then your mind will move as a unity.

13. The cause of all the trouble in your life is due to the kind of company you are keeping in your mind. Take inventory now.

14. Your thought and feeling create your destiny. There is no one to blame but yourself.

15. People create their own hell and their own heaven, here and now, by the way they think all day long.

16. Retribution or reward depends on how you use your mind. The law of action and reaction is universal throughout nature. Think good; good follows. Think evil; evil follows.

LAW 7

THE WONDERFUL LAW
OF SECURITY

Do you feel secure or insecure? The answer depends primarily on your basic approach to life. Dr. William Y., a distinguished research physician associated with the University of California at Los Angeles, told me the other day that he has never found a patient with a strong sense of security who suffers from chronic worry, fear complexes, or mental disorders of any kind. He attributed this sense of security to an abiding faith and trust in a Supreme Power that watches over us in all our ways.

If you have not learned about your own essential greatness and the infinite riches within you, you tend to magnify the problems and the difficulties that confront you. You empower them, giving them influence and control that you fail to attribute to yourself. One of the main reasons for your feeling of insecurity is that you are regarding the externals of life as causes, not realizing that they are really effects.

HOW TO GET THE FEELING OF SECURITY

There is no real security apart from your sense of oneness with God—the Source of all blessings. This is the first thing you have to realize. By applying the principles described in this book, you can develop a practical, workable, sane, and marvelous feeling of inner security. There is an urge within each of us that cries out for union with an Eternal Source. Join now with this Infinite Power, and you will immediately draw upon its strength.

You are immersed in an infinite ocean of Life—the Infinite Mind—which permeates you entirely and in which you live, move, and have your being. Remember that this Infinite Power has never been defeated or frustrated by anything outside itself. This Infinite Power is omnipotent, and when you consciously unite with it through your thought and feeling, you immediately become greater than that which you feared.

The Infinite lies stretched in smiling repose within you; this is the true state of your mind. The power and wisdom of this Infinite Mind become potent and active in your life the moment you recognize its existence and establish your mental contact with it. If you do this now, you will immediately experience a marvelous feeling of inner security, and you will discover the peace that passeth understanding.

HE STOPPED PRAYING
AGAINST HIMSELF

A friend of mine, Ernest S., was involved in a prolonged lawsuit that had cost him a considerable sum of money in legal fees. His attorney told him he would probably lose the case. This meant that Ernest would be more or less penniless. He was terrified. While discussing the matter with me, he moaned that he had nothing left to live for. The only thing to do was to end it all.

"Do you have any idea how destructive it is to say things like that?" I demanded sternly. "Every time you think or say such negative thoughts, you help prolong the case that is wrecking your peace of mind. In effect, you are praying against yourself."

I then asked him a simple question. "What would you say if I told you this minute that there had been a perfect, harmonious solution and the whole matter was concluded?"

"I would be delighted and eternally grateful," he said. "I would feel like a man condemned to die who just received a pardon."

"Will you try to make your inner, silent thought conform to your desired aim?" I asked. "That, I firmly believe, is what will bring about a successful conclusion of this case."

"I'll try," he pledged.

I gave him a prayer to affirm regularly and systematically: "I give thanks for the perfect, harmonious solution that takes place through the wisdom of the All-Wise One."

Ernest repeated this prayer to himself often during the day, especially when difficulties, delays, setbacks, arguments, doubts, and fear came to his mind. He completely ceased making negative statements, and he also controlled his silent thoughts, knowing that his inner thought and feeling would always be made manifest.

It is what you feel on the inside that is made manifest. You can say one thing with your mouth and feel another way in your heart; it is what you feel on the inside that is reproduced on the screen of space.

Ernest learned through practice and discipline never to affirm inwardly anything he did not want to experience outwardly. His lips and his heart agreed on a harmonious solution to his legal case, and Divine Justice prevailed. Additional information was provided from a completely unexpected source, and the lawsuit was resolved so that Ernest did not suffer a financial loss.

My friend had realized that his security was dependent upon his alignment with the Infinite Presence, which moves as unity, harmony, justice, and right action. He discovered that nothing could oppose the Infinite Power that moves the world.

THE END OF MY ROPE

"I'm at the end of my rope," Celeste B. told me. An art student, she had been given my name by a friend who had attended some of my lectures. "I suffer from a serious blood disorder. The chances are, at some point I'll become an invalid for the rest of my life. Who'd want to hire someone like me, or get involved in a personal relationship? My life is over, before it even started!"

"You're certainly painting a very bleak picture," I said. "Who gave you that prognosis? Your physician? A specialist?"

She hesitated. "Well . . . no. In fact, my doctor does her best to sound encouraging. No, it's my relatives, and they ought to know. There was my Uncle Bob. He died of the same kind of condition. The doctors tried everything to cure him, but nothing worked. It's incurable. I'm just like him, I'm afraid."

"Why are you here?" I asked. "What do you hope to get from our talk?"

She looked down at the floor. "My friend said you might help heal me," she said softly.

"No, I'm afraid not," I replied. She stiffened. I quickly added, "But I may be able to help you heal yourself. Whatever medical problems your doctor has uncovered, they are being made worse because your subconscious mind is being saturated with your relatives' negative statements about your health. As long as you continue to listen to them, you are not likely to experience a healing. However, once you recall that you are not your uncle, that you are your own person, the Infinite Healing Presence that created your body can begin to heal its own handiwork."

After our consultation, Celeste began to use a different tone to her subconscious mind. I told her to slowly, quietly, lovingly, and feelingly affirm the following prayer:

The Creative Intelligence that made my body is now re-creating my blood. The Healing Presence knows how to heal, and it is transforming every cell of my body to God's perfect pattern. I hear and see the doctor telling me that I am whole. I have this picture now in my mind. I see her clearly and I hear her voice; she is saying to me, "Celeste, you are healed! It is a miracle!" I know that this constructive imagery is going down deep into my subconscious mind, where it is being developed and brought to pass. I know that the Infinite Healing Presence is now restoring me in spite of all sensory evidence to the contrary. I feel this, I believe it, and I am now identifying with my aim—perfect health.

Celeste repeated this prayer four or five times daily for ten or fifteen minutes, particularly before falling asleep at night. At times she found her mind falling back into its old habits of fretting, fussing, worrying, and recounting the verdicts of others. When these thoughts came to her mind, she learned to issue the order, "Stop! I am the master over all of my thoughts, imagery, and responses, and they must obey me. From now on, all of my thoughts are on God and His healing power. This is the way I feed my subconscious; I constantly identify with God, and my inner thought and feeling is 'Thank you, Father!' I do this a hundred times a day, or a thousand times, if necessary."

Within three months, Celeste's blood count had become nearly normal. By repetition, prayer, and meditation, she established new habits of positive thought, and she succeeded in aligning her subconscious mind with her desire. She proved the truth in the Bible, *Thy faith hath made thee whole* (Matt. 9:22).

SECURITY CANNOT
BE LEGISLATED

No government, however well-intentioned, can guarantee you peace, happiness, joy, abundance, or security. You cannot determine exactly all of the events, circumstances, and experiences through which you will pass on your life's journey. Unforeseen cataclysms, floods, earthquakes, typhoons, and monsoons will take place that destroy cities and properties and wipe out the holdings of thousands of people. Wars, insurrections, and political upheavals take place that have unpredictable effects on people and on their economies. International tragedies and fear of war have had catastrophic effects on the stock markets of the world.

All material possessions are vulnerable to change. There is no real security in stocks, bonds, or money in the bank. The value of a fifty-dollar bill depends on the integrity and honesty of our government and its ability to back up a sound currency. A check from a bank or from another person is only a piece of paper. Its value depends on the honesty and integrity of the writer of the check and on your faith in the soundness of the bank.

PRAY AND PROTECT
YOUR INVESTMENTS

If you devote some time and attention every day to scientific prayer and meditation, you will experience a changed mental attitude, and you cannot and will not suffer from the many hazards and unforeseen catastrophes that are referred to in this chapter.

Walk in the consciousness of God's eternal supply. Know in your heart that the Overshadowing Presence is watching over you in all your ways. Remember that as long as you maintain a prosperity consciousness, you cannot suffer losses. When you build into your mentality the awareness of the Eternal Source of supply, you cannot become impoverished. No matter what form wealth takes, you will always be amply supplied.

PRAYER CONTROLLED HIS UPS AND DOWNS

"Two months ago, I was worth a fortune," Eric W. told me over lunch. "Then all the dot-coms I'd put my money in tanked, one after the other. Now I'm reduced to wondering if my credit card will be refused when I try to pay for this meal. And health . . . One month I'm hiking the Sierras, and the next I can hardly hobble up the stairs in my house. Isn't there anything I can do to even out all these swings?"

"Of course," I told him. "Anyone can achieve a balanced life in which serenity and tranquility reign supreme. The key is to work to acquire mental and emotional control. You'll find that you can preserve your equanimity regardless of circumstances. It's as Marcus Aurelius said, almost two thousand years ago: *Nothing happens to any man which he is not formed by nature to bear.* In Hawaii, a guide will show you a hut where the great writer, Robert

Louis Stevenson, wrote a masterpiece, *Treasure Island*, despite the fact that he was suffering from an acute case of tuberculosis!"

I gave Eric a spiritual prescription to follow that would help him find strength and assurance from the kingdom of God within him. He prayed frequently during each day, dwelling on these eternal verities:

Thou wilt keep him in perfect peace, whose mind is stayed on thee: because he trusteth in thee (Isa. 26:3). I know that the inner desires of my heart come from God within me. God wants me to be happy. God's will for me is life, love, truth, and beauty. I mentally accept my good now, and I become a perfect channel for the divine. I am an expression of God. I am divinely directed in all my ways, and I am always in my true place, doing the thing I love to do. I refuse to accept as truth the opinions of others, for my mind is a part of God's mind, and I am always reflecting divine wisdom and divine intelligence. God's ideas unfold within my mind in perfect sequence. I am always poised, balanced, serene, and calm, for I know that God always will reveal to me the perfect solution to all my needs. The Lord is my shepherd; I shall not want for any good thing. I am divinely active and divinely creative. I sense and feel the rhythm of God. I hear the melody of God whispering its message of love to me.

HOW SHE HEALED HER SENSE OF LOSS

A young woman named Daphne W. was brought to meet me after a service. "I've lost everything I ever lived for," she told me. "My father died last month. We were not very close, but I always expected him to be there. Then his lawyer told me that he had made some terrible investments over the past couple of years. I was always led to believe I would inherit a fortune, but it's all gone."

Daphne felt a deep sense of loss, and she feared the future. But fear can always be replaced by faith in God and all things good, once we know how to use our minds. In talking to Daphne, I explained that she could never really lose anything unless she accepted the loss in her mind, as all experiences take place through the mind.

Imagine that I have "lost" my watch. All this really means is that it is somewhere, but I can't find it just now. It may have fallen on the street, or perhaps I left it in a phone booth, or it may be that a pickpocket has it. Whatever has become of it, the watch is not lost in the Infinite Mind of God. *They shall not hurt nor destroy in all my holy mountain* (Isa. 11:9). Infinite Mind permeates and indwells every particle of matter in the universe. The watch is an idea in Mind, and even if my watch was run over by a truck and ground into dust, the human mind can create millions of watches. God cannot lose anything.

Daphne decided to heal her fear of loss and her deep sense of insecurity, which had caused her so much mental anguish. Her first step was to acquire an understanding of a law of mind, which is that no one can rob us of our good without our mental consent, by fearing or believing in loss. The second step was to make a definite mental choice, knowing that her choice of God's riches and wealth, when given attention and steadily adhered to, would be accepted by her subconscious mind and brought to pass in her experience.

Her third step was to remain faithful to the idea that God's wealth was flowing into her experience, knowing in her heart that her belief in God's promises would result in fulfillment.

This attitude of mind rapidly dissolved her sense of loss. Her mind began to move with God's mind, in one direction. How incongruous and ludicrous it would be to assume that the Infinite Mind of God could move in two directions at once!

Affirming the following prayer became Daphne's fourth step:

> *In quietness and in confidence shall be your strength* (Isa. 30:15). I know that my inner feeling of security is based on my knowledge that God takes care of me. I have confidence in His direction. My greatest security is that I know and feel God's Presence. I know deep down in my heart that God is the source of all life and all blessings. God is with me and for me. He watches over me, He cares for me, He provides for me, He supports me, and He loves me. My thoughts are thoughts of fulfillment, since all of God's desires are always being fulfilled. He restoreth my soul and my thought-life. His goodness and mercy follow me all the days of my life, for I have chosen to dwell mentally and spiritually with God all the days of my life.

After having prayed in this manner for six weeks, Daphne was invited to attend a political reception in Los Angeles. An important legislator was deeply impressed by her poise, self-assurance, and inner sense of tranquillity. She offered Daphne an important post on her staff in Sacramento. Daphne's belief in the fulfillment of her prayer brought results.

Life is always eminently fair. The ups and downs, sickness, turmoil, strife, and misfortune that at times beset our existence are the consequences of our misuse of the laws of mind and the results of our false and superstitious beliefs.

BUILDING A GLORIOUS FUTURE

Go to work on your thoughts, tune in to the Infinite One, and affirm boldly, [*I*] *shalt compass me about with songs of deliverance* (Psalms 32:7). Almightly God is within you. You are equipped to lead a glorious and wonderful life, for all the power of God is available to you. Release His wisdom, power, and glory in your life.

If you don't use your muscles, they will inevitably atrophy. You have mental and spiritual "muscles" that must also be exercised. If your thoughts, attitudes, motivations, and reactions are not God-like, your contact with God is broken, and you become depressed, rejected, fearful, morose, and morbid.

Look within. *The kingdom of God is within you* (Luke 17:21). God's power, wisdom, and strength to meet any and all challenges are within you. *The people that do know their God shall be strong, and do exploits* (Dan. 11:32). *Behold, I am the Lord, the God of all flesh: is there any thing too hard for me?* (Jer. 32:27).

A HEALTHY REVIEW

1. Your worries and fears really are due to your failure to align yourself with the Infinite, which knows no fear or opposition.

2. No real security can take place apart from your feeling of oneness with God.

3. Your inner, silent thought must agree with your aims in life; otherwise, your prayer can't be answered.

4. When you are constantly mentally denying what you are affirming outwardly, you cannot receive a healing.

5. A real sense of security is not dependent upon bonds, stocks, and real estate. The real feeling of security is based on faith and trust in God, the Giver of all gifts.

6. A government cannot guarantee security, peace, or happiness. You decree your own security, peace, joy, and health through the laws of your mind.

7. You protect your investments by knowing that all your possessions are watched over by the Overshadowing Presence, and you dwell constantly in the Secret Place.

8. Avoid ups and downs by realizing that divine law and order govern your life, and that God thinks, speaks, acts, and directs all your undertakings. Make a habit of this prayer, and poise and balance will be yours.

9. Fear can be replaced by faith in God and His eternal supply. *In quietness and in confidence shall be your strength* (Isa. 30:15).

10. You can lead a glorious and wonderful life by joining up with God and by knowing that God's power, wisdom, and strength are there to meet all problems. When you begin, God begins. *I and my Father are one* (John 10:30).

LAW 8

THE MAGICAL LAW OF MENTAL NUTRITION

I have known people who have had the choicest food and a perfectly balanced diet, according to the laws of nutrition, and yet they developed ulcers, cancer, arthritis, and other destructive and degenerative diseases.

The food of your experiences, conditions, and events is your thought-life. Your habitual thinking nourishes and sustains your conditions and causes them to increase and magnify in your experience. Fear thoughts, worry and critical thoughts, and angry and hateful thoughts are the food of sickness, despondence, failure, and misery.

All living creatures follow their food. Explorers and scientists tell us that in parts of the globe where food is unobtainable, there is no animal life. Life abounds where food is plentiful. When you feed your mind with negative food, sickness, lack, misery, and suffering come into your life, because they seek their food.

YOU ARE WHAT YOU MENTALLY EAT

All of us have heard the expression, "You are what you eat." If an idea is true, it is generally true in more than one sense. You are what you eat psychologically and spiritually. Thoughts of God, thoughts of love, kindness, optimism, joy, and good will are the foods of health, joy, happiness, and success. If you mentally absorb and digest a bountiful supply of these foods, you will attract and experience all these things in your life.

If you are hateful, envious, jealous, and full of hostility, the physical food you eat may well be transformed from health-giving to poisonous. On the other hand, if you are full of good will and eat the food on the table with joy and thanksgiving, it will be transmuted into beauty, vitality, wholesomeness, and strength. The bread or meat you eat becomes your flesh and blood. This is the inner meaning of the saying, "You are what you eat."

THE IMPORTANCE OF DIET

Food for the body is very important. Today, some of our foremost research physicians are pointing out the dangers of excessive fat, which interferes with the mechanical efficiency of all our vital organs, such as the heart, lungs, liver, and kidneys. We know that many physical and mental diseases can result from lack of certain vitamins and chemicals. Beriberi, a disease characterized by multiple inflammatory changes in the nerves, producing great muscular debility, is brought about by an insufficiency of vitamin B. We are all familiar with the need for sufficient calcium for pregnant women. Deficiency of vitamin A has deleterious effects on the eyes, and a sufficient amount of protein is essential for our well-being.

All this is important, but our mental and spiritual diet is of the greatest importance.

THE BREAD OF LOVE AND PEACE

I know a man, Donald L., who is the author of a wonderful book on nutrition. It is quite scientific and very sound. However, he himself suffers from acute ulcers. His physician tried to treat his condition with a course of antibiotics, linked with a special diet, but the ulcers only worsened.

When Donald described his situation in a conversation with me, I asked, "Have you noticed anything in your mental or emotional life that seems to be connected to the ulcers?"

"My life?" he replied. "Not at all. But I'll tell you one thing. I can't pick up a newspaper or watch a newscast without feeling a pang. All the top stories are about suffering, crime, injustice, and inhumanity. It makes me livid. I must spend a couple of hours every day writing letters and e-mails to people in Congress and the government, telling them exactly what I think about their actions."

"I take it you don't think very highly of them," I said dryly. "Would it be fair to call these angry messages?"

"Certainly," Donald said "and every bit of my anger is justified."

"Even the part that is responsible for your illness?" I asked. "You know, when you allow negative energy to build up inside yourself, it has an effect, even if you discharge much of it on an external target. If you want to be cured of your stomach condition, you will have to change your mental and emotional diet."

By the end of our talk, Donald had committed himself to adopting a new mental regimen:

> I am going to transform all negative impressions that come to
> me during the day. From now on, I will never permit news,
> propaganda, criticism, or negative statements of others to pro-
> mote negative reactions in me. When I am tempted to react
> negatively and vindictively, I will stop immediately and affirm
> to myself boldly, "God thinks, speaks, and acts through me
> now. His river of peace floods my mind and heart, and I am
> identified with my aim, which is peace and harmony."

As this new way of reacting became a habit, he began to feast on the bread of love and peace. He had a remarkable healing in a short period of time.

YOUR MENTAL AND SPIRITUAL DIET

The Bible says, *Thou shalt not eat any abominable thing* (Deut. 14:3). The inner, spiritual meaning of this is that you should not entertain or enthrone in your mind negative thoughts such as resentment, ill will, cynicism, hate, or anger.

Distinguished research physicians and other scientists point out that we have a new body every eleven months. You are creating new cells all the time. If you fill your mind with the eternal verities and spiritual values of life, your brain will send these spiritual vibrations all over your body through the medium of your nervous system. All the new cells will take on the vibrations of these spiritual overtones so that, like Job, you will be able to say: *Yet in my flesh shall I see God.* (Job 19:26)

To flourish and thrive, you need a special mental and spiritual diet. You are fed daily through the five senses by an avalanche of sights, sounds, and sundry concepts, both good and bad. Most of this food is highly unsavory. You must learn to turn inward to God and be replenished from the standpoint of Truth. Affirm frequently with feeling: "God is guiding me now. God's love fills my soul, God inspires me, and God illumines my pathway in life. I radiate love and good will to all. Divine law and order govern my life at all times."

This prayer is a wonderful spiritual diet for your mind. Wonders will happen as you make a habit of saying this prayer.

HER HEAD KNOWLEDGE BECAME HEART KNOWLEDGE

Romola D. came up to speak to me after a meeting in San Francisco. "I have read every book I can find on mental healing," she said. "I've even written articles on the subject myself. Yet I have not managed to heal myself of chronic colitis. How do you explain that?"

As we talked, I realized that Romola failed to meditate and reflect on what she read and wrote about the healing powers of the subconscious mind so that it would be incorporated into her subconscious mind.

She had studied different religions of the world, had read a vast number of inspirational books, had studied numerology and astrology, and seemed to be a charter member of every new and strange cult. She was so muddled, perplexed, and confused that her spiritual quest had left her mentally and emotionally disoriented.

I outlined a simple plan for her. I suggested she select what is eternally true, and that all her reading, thought-life, instruction, and decisions must meet and conform to the following standard:

> *Whatsoever things are true, whatsoever things are honest, whatsoever things are just, whatsoever things are pure, whatsoever things are lovely, whatsoever things are of good report; if there be any virtue, and if there be any praise, think on these things (Phil. 4:8).*

Romola accepted this spiritual standard. It enabled her to choose what is noble and God-like for the sanctuary of her own mind. Anything and everything that did not conform to this spiritual standard was positively and definitely rejected as unfit for the house of God, her own mind. She meditated on the following prayer five or six times daily:

> *He that dwelleth in the secret place of the most High shall abide under the shadow of the Almighty (Ps. 91:1). I dwell in*

the secret place of the most High; this is my own mind. All the thoughts I entertain conform to harmony, peace, and good will. My mind is the dwelling place of happiness, joy, and a deep sense of security. All the thoughts that enter my mind contribute to my joy, peace, and general welfare. I live, move, and have my being in the atmosphere of good fellowship, love, and unity.

All the people who dwell in my mind are God's children. I am at peace in my mind with all the members of my household and all humankind. The same good I wish for myself, I wish for all people. I am living in the house of God now. I claim peace and happiness, for I know I dwell in the house of the Lord forever.

Gradually, Romola's head knowledge of God's ideas became heart knowledge, and her chronic colitis faded away.

HIS MENTAL IMAGERY HEALED HIM

I was taken to meet a man in New York City, Al T., who never left his apartment. He would not go out into the street or even down to the lobby of the building. Whenever he planned to leave home, he would imagine all the dire things that might happen to him. He would feel faint and dizzy. This condition is called agoraphobia. The fear originated in Al's early childhood. When he was about five years old, he wandered away from home and was lost in the woods for several hours. His memory of being lost and the anxiety ensuing from it were still lurking in his subconscious mind.

Al freed himself by using his imagination correctly. At my suggestion, he began to spend about ten minutes, three times a day, imagining he was taking a bus, reading in the park, visiting stores, entering the library, buying groceries, or calling on friends. He began to feel the reality of all this.

Gradually, these constructive images penetrated the deeper layers of his subconscious mind and expunged from his deeper mind the fear pattern lodged there for several years. What he imagined and felt as true came to pass.

THE THANKFUL HEART

Use the following prayer frequently, and you will find yourself close to God, and all the food that you eat will be transmuted into beauty:

> I give supreme recognition to the God-Presence within me. I sincerely and honestly give thanks for all the blessings received. I give thanks for all the good in my life; I live in the feeling of grateful rejoicing. My thankful heart strikes the magic of the Divine response. Every day of my life I express thanks for my knowledge of the laws of mind and the way of the Spirit. I know that thankfulness is a movement of the heart first, which is followed by a movement of the lips. My uplifted heart opens up the treasure-house of Infinity within me and bespeaks my faith in the fulfillment of my prayers. I am truly thankful because I have found God in the midst of me. *I sought the Lord, and he heard me, and delivered me from all my fears* (Ps. 34:4). Anyone who possesses a thankful heart is always in tune with the Infinite and cannot suppress the joy that arises from contemplating God and His Holy Presence. In everything, I give thanks.

HIGHLIGHTS TO RECALL

1. The food of your experiences, conditions, and events is your thought-life.

2. All living creatures follow their food. Sickness, misery, pain, and suffering follow negative mental attitudes, because they seek their food.

3. You are what you eat psychologically and spiritually. Eat your food with joy and thanksgiving.

4. Food for the body is important, but our mental and spiritual diet is of supreme importance.

5. You can mentally transform all negative impressions that come to you through your five senses. Start now!

6. You have a new body every eleven months. Fill your mind with the eternal verities and you will become rejuvenated and revitalized.

7. Intellectual assent is not enough. The truths you accept consciously must be emotionalized and felt as true to be assimilated by the subconscious mind.

8. Your head knowledge must be incorporated into your subconscious mind (the heart); then your head knowledge will become heart knowledge, and your prayers will be answered.

9. You take a vacation from fear when you focus your attention on whatsoever things are true, noble,

lofty, and God-like. When fear thoughts knock at the door of your mind, let faith in God open the door, and there is no one there.

10. Fear is based on distorted, twisted imagination. Imagine you are doing the thing you are afraid to do, and the death of fear is certain.

11. The thankful heart is always close to God. Be thankful, and bless His Name.

LAW 9

THE GREAT LAW
OF LOVE

If you want to remain healthy, vigorous, and strong, you have to realize that there is but one Power, indivisible, and its source is love. This Power has no opposition. It is the omnipotent Life Principle that has overcome every opposition in this world. It goes on conquering and is forever victorious. Realize that you are one with this God-Power. You are aligned with it now, and mighty forces come to your aid.

LOVE IS ALWAYS OUTGOING

Love must have an object. Love is an emotional attachment. You can fall in love with music, art, a great project, a cause, or with your ideal. You can become emotionally attracted to the eternal verities. You can become absorbed and engrossed in science and many other things.

Einstein loved the principle of mathematics, so it revealed its secrets to him. That is what love does. Astronomers fall in love with the science of astronomy, and they are constantly revealing the secrets of the heavens to us.

HOW MUCH DO YOU WANT TO BE A NEW PERSON?

Do you want to leave your old self, with your false concepts and misleading ideas? Are you willing to espouse new ideas, new imagery, new viewpoints? Are you open and receptive? If you are, you must give up your resentments, grudges, peeves, fears, jealousies, and hates. Suppose you wanted to go from Los Angeles to New York. The first, absolutely necessary step would be to leave Los Angeles. In a similar way, if you want to be a new person, you must first give up your fears and hates. You must focus your attention on the concepts of harmony, health, peace, joy, love, and good will in order to enter into the joy of living.

WHY AN ACTOR FAILED THREE TIMES

Sean R. made an appointment to consult me. He told me, "I'm an actor. Next week I have a chance to break through to the sort of career I've always dreamed of. But I know I'm going to fail."

"What makes you so certain you'll fail?" I asked. "You were given this chance for some reason, weren't you?"

"I happen to be the right type for the part," he replied. "But I've auditioned before for important roles. Three times. Each time, I had this feeling that I was bound to screw up, and each time, someone else got the part. So you see? The feeling is accurate."

"That's one way to look at it," I said. "Another way is to realize that your feeling, your vivid imagination, was centered on failure. Nothing comes of nothing. Failure has many parents, but one of them, perhaps the most important, is the conviction that failure is inevitable."

"Are you saying I failed *because* I thought I was going to fail?" Sean asked. "I never thought of it that way before. Yet when you say it, it seems so obvious!"

"If you want to let your talent blossom," I said, "you will have to give up your connection to failure. You will have to let yourself become emotionally attached to a new view of yourself, a successful view."

HIS PRAYER OF TRIUMPH

At my suggestion, Sean isolated himself in his room, where he would not be disturbed, three or four times a day. He settled himself comfortably in his armchair and relaxed his body to the utmost. This physical inertia rendered his mind more receptive to his affirmations. For about five minutes at each sitting, he focused his mind on this affirmation:

I am completely relaxed and at ease. I am poised, serene, and calm. At the audition I act beautifully, majestically, and gloriously. The director congratulates me. I am at peace in my mind.

Sean followed this technique every day for about a week, particularly at night before going to sleep. When the time came for the audition he had once so feared, he performed every bit as successfully as he had seen in his affirmation. He was cast in the part, and the film turned out to be the first step in what has become a successful career.

LOVE OF GOD AND WHAT IT MEANS

The words *God* and *good* are synonymous. When you mentally and emotionally unite with honesty, integrity, justice, good will, and happiness, you are loving God, because you are loving that which is good. You are loving God when you are fascinated, absorbed, and captivated by the great truth that God is One and Indivisible. To love God is to give your allegiance, loyalty, and devotion to the One Power, refusing to recognize any other power in the world. When you definitely recognize and completely accept in your mind that God really is omnipotent, in the most practical, literal, and matter-of-fact manner, you are loving God, because you are loyal to the One Power. Sit down quietly at times and think over this vital, fascinating, and greatest of all truths. God is the only Power, and everything we are aware of is part of His self-expression.

LOVE AND FEAR CANNOT DWELL TOGETHER

I was giving a series of lectures at Caxton Hall in London when a young woman named Beatrice W. came backstage to speak to me. She told me she had recently finished the course of study at a famous acting school. She went on, "I heard you say love and fear can't dwell together. I love the theater, but I am full of fear. I am afraid that I am unworthy, that my talent is too limited. Do I dare waste the time of directors at tryouts? There are so many others who have better qualifications."

"It sounds to me as if you have given your allegiance to a very small idea of yourself," I replied. "If I were to show you a nobler, sweeter, grander concept of yourself, do you think you could welcome and embrace it? It is right there, longing for your attention and care. It suffers from your neglect like an orphaned child, and *you* suffer as well, like a parent who has lost a child."

Beatrice's eyes filled with tears. "How terribly sad!" she exclaimed. "Yes, of course. I will take it in and love it. Does it have a name?"

"Yes," I told her. "Its name is your Greater Self, the God-Presence within you."

Beatrice began to meditate on the fact that she possessed almost illimitable possibilities of development. She acknowledged powers within her that had never been released. She began to affirm regularly and systematically:

I can do all things through the God-Power that flows through me. God thinks, speaks, and acts through me, and I am a wonderful and successful actor. The Infinite is always successful, and I am one with the Infinite. I am a child of God, and what is true of Him is true of me. When fear and worry thoughts come into my mind, I banish them with the knowledge that God's love fills my soul and God is with me now.

Since that day, Beatrice's career has flourished. God's power captivated her imagination. It thrilled her through and through, and she became entranced with the idea of being a great actor. This love caused her to unite with her ideal. She did not try to hold the ideal. The ideal captivated her; that is love. Then all fear went away. Fear was swallowed up in love, because love and fear cannot dwell together.

LOVE CONQUERS JEALOUSY

Shakespeare wrote, "Oh, beware of jealousy; it is the green-eyed monster, which doth mock the meat it feeds on." Milton wrote, "Jealousy is the injured lover's hell." Jealous people poison their own banquets and then eat them. Jealousy is a mental poison, and its cause is fear. The jealous person demands exclusive devotion and is intolerant of rivalry. Furthermore, the jealous person is suspiciously watchful regarding the fidelity of husband, wife, lover, or friend. Basically, jealousy arises from a deep-seated fear or mistrust of another plus a feeling of guilt and uncertainty about oneself.

A man named Steven P. told me his wife was insanely jealous. "Every time I turn around, she's accusing me of having affairs with other women," he said. "I can't swear I've never been attracted to anyone else, though I've certainly never done anything underhanded. But Joyce is absolutely sure she has an unknown rival."

"What makes her so certain, if she's totally wrong?" I asked.

He laughed bitterly. "She has an infallible source of information," he said. "It's called a Ouija board!"

At Steven's request, I had a conference with his wife. I explained to her in detail that it was her own subconscious mind that was confirming her suspicion and resentment toward her husband. She began to see clearly that it was her deeper mind that, through imperceptible movements of her fingers, operated the Ouija board. In other words, she was simply talking to herself.

Fortunately, Joyce was honest enough to see her error. Both she and her husband made a commitment to send forth thoughts of love, peace, and kindliness to one another. This good will dissolved the negative attitudes and brought peace where discord and suspicion had reigned. The explanation was the cure. This woman learned to trust her husband, and where love and trust exist, there is no jealousy.

THE LORD GIVETH THE INCREASE

The scientific thinker substitutes the word *law* for *Lord* in the Bible. This is the law of your subconscious mind, which magnifies whatever you deposit in it. It is an impersonal law of cause and effect.

I recently explained the meaning of the phrase "the Lord giveth the increase" to a local real estate broker named Josh B. He had not made a sale in two months. The reason was that he was giving more and more of his attention to the negative aspects of his situation. Gradually his condition got very much worse, and he suffered from loss of prestige, health, and finances; sickness in his family; and finally, no business at all.

Josh discovered it was far more fascinating, alluring, and captivating to contemplate success, harmony, wealth, peace of mind, more satisfied customers, and better service to his clients. I gave him the following prayer, which I suggested he repeat out loud, slowly, quietly, and lovingly, five or six times a day until he reconditioned his mind to success and wealth:

> I believe in my heart that I can predict for myself harmony, health, peace, prosperity, and success in business. I enthrone the concepts of peace, harmony, guidance, success, and prosperity in my mind now. I know and believe these thoughts (seeds) will grow and manifest themselves in my experience. I am a gardener; as I sow, so shall I reap. I sow God-like thoughts (seeds), and these wonderful seeds of success, harmony, prosperity, peace, and good will automatically will bring forth a wonderful harvest. I nourish and sustain these seeds regularly and systematically by thinking with interest on them. I know my subconscious mind is a bank that multiplies and magnifies whatever I deposit. I will draw out the fruit of the wonderful seeds I am depositing now. I make these thoughts real by feeling the reality of them. I believe in

the law of increase in the same manner that seeds deposited in the soil come forth multiplied thirtyfold, sixtyfold, and hundredfold. Like seeds, my thoughts dwell in the darkness of my subconscious mind and, like the seeds, they come above the ground (become objectified) as conditions, experiences, and events. I think frequently on these things, and God's power is with my thoughts of good. God giveth the increase.

When fear or worry thoughts came to him, Josh immediately countered them by affirming, "God giveth the increase along all lines." At the end of a month, he was back in his old stride, with more business than he could handle.

HOW SHE PASSED HER EXAMINATION

"Your lectures saved my life!" Agnes H. told me. She was a college student who had attended several meetings about the powers of the subconscious mind. "I was facing junior comps—that's a three-hour exam that is sheer murder. The day before, just thinking about it made my knees start trembling with fear. I just knew I was going to bomb the exam, like totally!"

"But you didn't," I said with a smile.

Her eyes widened. "How did you know! That is so amazing! No, I didn't. I even pulled a 'high pass,' and the reason was that I remembered what you said about fear, that it was a signal to do something. I made up my mind to overcome it by reversing it."

"Good thought," I said. "How did you set about it?"

"I reasoned with myself," she explained. "I repeated to myself, 'The Lord is my shepherd. God can't be afraid. God is right here. God is my peace and my strength. His river of peace flows through me. God's love indwells me and casts out all fear. I am at peace. The poise and harmony of God is here. I am relaxed, and I answer all questions in divine order. Infinite Intelligence reveals to me everything I need to know.' It worked!"

By practicing the law of substitution, Agnes eradicated her fear with her faith in God and the good. She did not stay frozen at the end of the pendulum of fear. She conquered her fear and passed her examination with high marks.

FEAR THOUGHTS CAN'T HURT YOU

Fear thoughts, worry thoughts, or negative thoughts of any kind will not hurt you unless you entertain them for a long period of time and emotionalize them deeply. Otherwise, they will flow through you without doing the least damage. Potentially they may be trouble, but only if you allow them to become actualized. Your fears cannot be actualized unless you emotionalize them. At that stage, you begin to impress your subconscious mind, and whatever is impressed in the subconscious mind will come to pass.

BECOME A SPIRITUAL GIANT

Your fear is an aggressive, domineering thought or idea that brags about its power and intimidates, bullies, browbeats, and frightens you into submission to its unrighteous reign. Perhaps you are afraid to meet this gangster in your mind. Maybe you are afraid of the results, and you hesitate to meet this sinister gangster and rout it out.

Fear is a shadow of the mind held by ignorance and darkness. When you hold your fear up to the light of reason and intelligence, it cannot stand the light, and it disappears.

Your state of mind is your master. It is foolish to let that ignorant, blind, stupid monster *fear* push you around and direct your activities. Consider yourself too smart, too brilliant for that to happen. Your faith in God is greater than fear. Fear is faith upside down. Fear is a conglomeration of dark and sinister shadows in the mind. In short, fear is faith in the wrong thing. Become a spiritual giant, call forth confidence in God, and summon His force and power.

When you go forth in the assurance that "one with God is a majority," you will find yourself watched over and guided in every way, and you will became the inevitable victor.

LOST IN THE JUNGLE

When I was about ten years old, I became lost in the jungle. At first I was terrified. Then I began to claim that God would lead me out and take care of me. I was immediately seized with an overpowering hunch to travel in a certain direction. This inner push or tendency of the subconscious—which I followed—proved to be correct. I was miraculously led into the arms of a searching party after two days' time. This lead was the prompting of my subconscious mind, which knew the way out of the jungle.

In using your subconscious mind, remember that it reasons deductively. It sees the end only, thereby bringing to a logical, sequential conclusion the nature of the premise in the conscious mind.

DON'T FIGHT FEAR

Don't fight fear with fear; instead, meet it with a direct declaration of God's Presence and Power, which render fear powerless. Say to yourself, "The Lord is the strength of my life; of whom should I be afraid?"

Are you afraid of some disease that has gripped you? You will notice that an erroneous thought in your mind can brag and boast of its pseudo strength, and it intimidates you. Don't let such thoughts bully and browbeat you. Meet and subdue them now. Realize that all disease is manufactured by your own mind; it is not something you catch on the outside.

You can change your mind by realizing that the Infinite Healing Presence that made your body is healing it now. As you do this consciously and knowingly, there will be a rearrangement of the thought patterns in your subconscious, and a healing will follow. Your present conviction determines your future and your experience.

THE ENEMY IN HER OWN MIND

"I'm so mad at Mary, I could practically kill her!" The young woman who made this rather alarming declaration was Bernadette D., an associate in a large law firm, who had come to me for counseling. "She does nothing but spread lies about me. I swear, some days I can't seem to think of anything else but her evil machinations."

"You mean that Mary is controlling your thoughts?" I asked.

Bernadette blinked and paused. "Er—not exactly. Sort of."

"More than 'sort of,' from what you say," I remarked. "You've permitted this person to disturb you. You've given her power over you."

As we talked, Bernadette came to understand that her trouble was in her own thought-life. Mary was not responsible for the way she was thinking about her. No, the source of the problem was in Bernadette's own mental imagery and thought patterns. She allowed fear to run riot in her mind, intimidating, bullying, and frightening her. Yet the whole process was her own creation. The enemy, fear, was really of her own making.

Bernadette decided to chop off the head of this fear-thought with the sword of spiritual reason. She saturated her mind with the simple truth, "God is, and His Presence fills my soul and rules my life." She refused to permit Mary to give her migraine attacks, indigestion, insomnia, or the jitters. She realized the power was in her own thought-life and she was the one who determined how her thoughts moved. It dawned on her that no one else had the power to upset her or to take away her faith and confidence in God and all things good.

Bernadette had a complete healing of the mind. Her favorite prayer became:

> God in action in my life brings me beauty, peace, divine right place, and harmony. I am the offspring of the Infinite and a child of Eternity. I draw close to God, my Heavenly Father. He loves me and cares for me. As I turn to Him, He turns to me; then the dawn appears and all the shadows flee.

LOVE'S HEALING BALM

Here is a wonderful prayer for casting out fear. Affirm these truths frequently, and you will find that an inner sense of peace and tranquillity will come over you:

> The love of God flows through me now; I am surrounded by the peace of God, and all is well. Divine love surrounds, enfolds, and encompasses me. This Infinite love is inscribed in my heart and written in my inward parts. I radiate love in thought, words, and deeds. Love unifies and harmonizes all the powers, attributes, and qualities of God within me. Love means joy, peace, freedom, bliss, and praise. Love is free-

dom. It opens prison doors and sets free all the captives. I am radiating love toward all, for everyone represents the love of God. I salute the Divinity in the other. I know and believe that divine love heals me now. Love is a guiding principle in me; it brings into my experience perfect, harmonious relationships. *God is love;* and *he that dwelleth in love dwelleth in God, and God in him* (1 John 4:16).

BASIC POINTS TO REMEMBER

1. Love is an emotional attachment. Love must have an object.

2. If you really want to banish fear, you must give up your jealousies, hatreds, peeves, and grudges.

3. Get a new estimate and blueprint of yourself. Fall in love with your Greater Self.

4. Love of God means that you are mentally and emotionally tied with that which is lovely, pure, noble, and God-like. You honor only one Power.

5. Love is faith and loyalty to God. Fear is faith in the wrong thing. Fear is a shadow in the mind. Love and fear can't dwell together.

6. A jealous person is full of fear and feels insecure and unworthy. Love and trust cast out jealousy.

7. Your subconscious magnifies everything you deposit in it. Deposit love, faith, confidence, laughter, and good will.

8. When your knees are shaking with fear, overcome the fear by realizing that God can't be afraid, and you are one with God.

9. Fear thoughts can't hurt you unless you indulge them and emotionalize them.

10. Fear is a thought you allow in your mind that browbeats and intimidates you. Enthrone love and faith in God in your mind.

11. When lost in the jungles of the earth or in a mental jungle of confusion and fear, realize that God knows the way out. He will answer you.

12. Don't fight fear with fear. Meet it with a direct declaration: "God is the only Presence and the only Power, and there is nothing to fear."

13. Chop off the head of your fear-thought with the sword of spiritual reason.

14. *He that dwelleth in love dwelleth in God, and God in him* (1 John 4:16).

LAW 10

THE POSITIVE LAW OF EMOTIONAL CONTROL

The ancient Greeks said, "Know thyself."* As you study yourself, you seem to be made up of four parts: your physical body, your emotional nature, your intellect, and your spiritual nature.

You are placed here to so discipline yourself that your intellectual, emotional, and physical natures are completely aligned, controlled, and directed along God-like ways.

Your physical body has no initiative of itself, no self-conscious intelligence, and no volition in and of itself. It is completely subject to your commands or decrees. Look upon your body as a great disk upon which you play your emotions and beliefs. Being a disk on which impressions of all sorts can be made, it will faithfully record all your emotionalized concepts and will never deviate from them. It will register equally well a melody of love and beauty, or

*Bartlett's, "Inscription at the Delphic Oracle," from Plutarch, Morals.

149

one of grief and sorrow. Resentment, jealousy, hatred, anger, and depression are all expressed in the body as various diseases. As you learn to control your mental and emotional nature, you will become a channel for the Divine, and you will release the imprisoned splendor concealed within you.

BECOMING EMOTIONALLY MATURE

Think this over for a moment: Even if you were the richest person in the world, you could not buy yourself a healthy body. Yet you can gain health through the riches of the mind, such as thoughts of peace, harmony, and perfect health.

It is absolutely essential for you to control your emotions if you want to become emotionally and spiritually mature. You are considered emotionally mature when you release your feelings constructively and harmoniously. If you do not discipline or bridle your emotions, you are considered emotionally immature and not grown-up, even though chronologically you may be fifty years old.

GETTING THE RIGHT CONCEPT OF YOURSELF

The greatest tyrant is a false idea that controls your mind and holds you in bondage. The ideas you hold about yourself induce definite emotions within you. Psychologically speaking, emotions control your course along life's path, for good or evil.

If you are full of resentment toward someone or are possessed by a grudge, these emotions will exert an evil influence over you and will govern your actions in a way that will be very different from what you may honestly desire. When you want to be friendly, affable, and cordial, you will be ugly, cynical, and sour. When you want to be healthy, successful, and prosperous in life, you will find everything going wrong.

Those of you who are reading this book are aware of your capacity to choose a concept of peace and good will. Sincerely accept the ideas of peace and love in your mind, and you will be governed, controlled, and guided accordingly.

HOW SHE OVERCAME DEPRESSION

"Last year, my only child died," Madeleine T. said. She had come to my office for a consultation. "Tony was only seven. The doctors did everything they could, but it was hopeless."

"I'm sorry," I said. "Your husband . . .?"

"I'm—I *was*—a single mother," she said. She looked away as her eyes filled with tears. "Tony was my whole world, and now that's gone. I don't know how I can go on. I have constant, terrible migraines that leave me dizzy and sick to my stomach. I had to stop driving because my vision became affected."

"How do you spend your time?" I asked. "Do you have a profession?"

"I am a qualified nurse," she replied. "But I haven't worked at it since Tony was born. About the only thing Tony's father did right was make it possible for me to live very frugally without working. I was able to spend all my time raising my son. If I hadn't had that time with him . . . "

"I honor and respect your grief," I said. "But clinging to it for too long will not benefit your son and does definite harm to you. I think on some level you realize that. That is the reason you sought this meeting, isn't it? A hope, perhaps unformulated, that with my help, you would find a way out of this terrible valley of the shadow that you find yourself trapped in?"

"I never thought . . .," Madeline began. "I'm here because my closest friend told me to come. But I'm the one who agreed, who decided. Yes, maybe you're right. Tony would be so sad to see what his loss has done to me. He was such a lively, cheerful boy. We had great fun together, even when he became too sick to leave his bed."

At the end of our talk, I suggested to Madeleine that she go to a hospital and offer her services in the children's ward. She followed my advice and, in offering her time at a local hospital, she began to pour out love on the children; she coddled, cossetted, and played with them. Her love was no longer bottled up within her. She again had someone who needed her, and she began to release the emotion of love along constructive channels.

She practiced what is called sublimation by redirecting

in God-like ways the energy that was locked up in her sub-conscious mind. In this manner, she drained off all the poison pockets in her deeper mind. She became joyous, happy, radiant, and free.

HOW SHE OVERCAME BAD TEMPER

A woman who had attended several of my public lectures on the power of the subconscious mind sought me out before the next lecture. She introduced herself as Marina R., then said, "I've always had a terrible temper, since I was a little girl. And lately . . . well! My new neighbors are impossible. They play loud music late at night, they leave their garbage cans uncovered for animals to turn over and rummage through, and they laugh if I say a word of reproach."

"You must find their behavior very trying," I said.

"That's not the half of it!" she proclaimed. "But I've found a way to deal with the situation without blowing my top. I understand, after listening to your lectures, that I mustn't allow my anger and hatred to poison my subconscious mind."

"And what is this way you've found?" I asked curiously.

Marina laughed. "It depends on the weather," she said. "If it's a nice day, I go dig in the garden. As I work, I say aloud to myself, 'I am digging in the garden of God and planting God's ideas.' If the weather isn't so good, I get a bucket and a roll of paper towels and wash the windows. As

I do, I say, 'I am cleansing my mind with the waters of love and life.' It works every time. Not only do I get over the temptation to become angry, but I put myself in a positive frame of mind *and* I get a few chores done!"

HIS MENTAL PHOTOGRAPH

Once, while crossing the English Channel from Dover to Calais, I had an interesting chat with a young man named Cyril R., who was studying mental discipline in Paris.

"Now and again," he said, "I stop and take a sort of mental photograph of my thoughts, sensations, moods, reactions, and even my tone of voice. If I find negatives among them, I tell myself, 'These are not of God; they are destructive and false. I will mentally turn to God within me and think from the standpoint of wisdom, truth, and beauty.'"

Cyril explained that he had made a habit of this. He would stop when he got angry and say to himself, "This is not the Infinite thinking, speaking, and acting in me. I now think, speak, and act from the standpoint of God and His love."

Every time Cyril was tempted to become angry, critical, depressed, or irritable, he would think of God and His love and peace, and the temptation would pass. This is internal discipline and spiritual understanding.

YOU CAN CONTROL
YOUR EMOTIONS

It is vital to grasp how our emotions are generated. Suppose you are walking down the street and you see someone who is terribly crippled. Your heart beats faster, you feel a sort of vise clutch at your chest, and you know that an emotion has been aroused in you. Your thought image tells you that the emotion is pity. But consider that someone else, who had never learned to pity the afflicted, might take that same arousal and interpret it as disgust.

You know that you cannot imagine an emotion, but if you imagine an episode or event of the past, you will at the same time recall the corresponding emotion. The first step, before you can induce an emotion, is to entertain a thought or mental image.

An emotion is always the working out of an idea in your mind. If you sincerely wish to govern and to control your emotions, you must maintain control over your thoughts and mental images.

By taking charge of your thoughts, you can substitute love for fear, good will for ill will, joy for sadness, and peace for disquiet. The instant you receive the stimulus of a negative emotion, supplant it with the mood of love and good will. Instead of giving way to fear, say to yourself, "One with God is a majority." Fill your mind with the concepts of faith, confidence, peace, and love; then the negative thoughts cannot enter.

THE EMOTION OF LOVE FREED HIM

While waiting for my flight at Kennedy Airport, I got into a conversation with an Air Force officer, Major Roger L. He told me he had just returned from a tour of duty patrolling the no-fly zone in southern Iraq. During every one of his missions, he knew that at any moment a ground-to-air missile might strike and destroy his plane with no warning or time to evade it.

"Weren't you afraid?" I asked.

"Going into combat, only a fool *isn't* afraid," he replied. "But I knew I had to conquer my fear, not allow it to conquer me. I had a powerful ally. I kept repeating to myself, 'God's love surrounds me and envelops this airplane. His love is my guide and my direction. He watches over me, and I am in His Presence.'"

This affirmation impressed Roger's subconscious mind with the feeling of love and faith. The mood of love superseded his fear. *Perfect love casteth out fear* (1 John 4:18).

HOW YOUR EMOTIONS AFFECT YOUR BODY

Have you noticed the effect of fear upon your face, eyes, heart, and other organs? You know the effect on your digestive tract of bad news or grief. Observe the change that takes place when it is found that the bad news is groundless.

All negative emotions are destructive and depress the vital forces of the body. Chronic worriers usually have trouble with digestion. If something very pleasant occurs in their experience, their digestion becomes normal, because normal circulation is restored and the necessary gastric secretions are no longer interfered with.

The way to overcome and discipline your emotions is not through repression or suppression. When you repress an emotion, the energy accumulates in your subconscious mind and remains snarled there. This occurs in the same manner as the pressure increases in a boiler when all the valves are closed and the heat of the fire is increased. In the end, there is a powerful explosion.

Today in the field of psychosomatics, it is being discovered that many cases of ill health, such as arthritis, asthma, cardiac troubles, and even failures in life, are due to suppressed or repressed emotions that may have occurred during early life or childhood. These repressed or suppressed emotions rise like ghosts to haunt you later on. However, techniques exist that can make you free of them for the rest of your life.

THE POSITIVE EMOTIONS OF FAITH AND CONFIDENCE

There is a spiritual and psychological way to follow in banishing the repressed or suppressed emotions inhabiting the gloomy gallery of your mind. The ideal way to rid yourself of these emotions is to practice the law of substitution. Through the law of mental substitution, you substitute a positive, constructive thought for the negative thought. When negative thoughts enter your mind, do not fight them. Just say to yourself: "My faith is in God and all things good. His love watches over me at all times." You will find the negative thoughts disappear just as light dispels the darkness.

If you are disturbed, anxious, or worried, meditate on the words of the Psalms and affirm:

> *The Lord is my shepherd; I shall not want* (Ps. 23:1).
> *I will fear no evil: for thou art with me* (Ps. 23:4).
> *God is . . . a very present help in trouble* (Ps. 46:1).
> *The Lord is my light and my salvation; whom shall I fear?*
> *the Lord is the strength of my life; of whom shall I be afraid?*
> (Ps. 27:1).

As you mentally dwell on these great truths, you will inevitably generate the positive emotions of faith and confidence that neutralize and destroy any negative emotion.

WATCH YOUR REACTIONS

I have known Bernard J. for years, since the time we were neighbors. The last time I saw him, I immediately noticed that his complexion was redder than it used to be. I asked him about this.

"My blood pressure, I guess," he told me. "I'm on medication, but I don't think it helps much."

Thinking back, I asked, "Do you still write so many letters to the newspapers and listen to all those call-in shows?"

"Of course I do," he retorted. "Somebody has to take all those idiots to task. I swear, either the whole world is getting stupider and stupider or it's simply that the media have been taken over by cretins!"

"Do you think there might be some connection between the way you react to them and your high blood pressure?" I asked.

"Oho!" he said. "I hear a sermon coming! No, quite seriously, I know I have not paid so much attention as I should to my spiritual growth. I mean to get to it. But first, I have to finish straightening out some of these dolts who have the nerve to call themselves commentators. Besides, you have to admit I'm usually right."

"Does it really matter?" I asked gently. "You know, it doesn't make the slightest difference if all those writers and commentators are wrong and you, alone, are right. The negative emotions that saturate your mind are destructive. They are robbing you of vitality, health, and peace of mind."

By the end of our discussion, Bernard decided that, from that moment forward, he would give all politicians, writers, commentators, newscasters, and talk show hosts the freedom and the right to say and to write whatever they believed was true. He accorded them the perfect right and freedom to express themselves according to the inner dictates of their hearts. He also decided that it was perfectly reasonable to assume that they would grant him the complete right and freedom to write articles or letters that were in complete disagreement with what they said and wrote. He realized that this was a sign of emotional maturity and that it had been childish for him to have resented and hated those who disagreed with his views.

He also adopted a simple prayer formula to help him keep his new resolution:

> From this moment forward, I will think right, feel right, act right, do right, and be right. I will think, speak, write, and react from the Divine Center within me and not from the superimposed structure of false beliefs, prejudices, bigotry, and ignorance. From the depths of my heart, I wish for all men the right to life, liberty, and the pursuit of happiness, and I practice the Golden Rule and the Law of Love.

By the end of the month, Bernard's blood pressure was down in the normal range. At his next physical, his doctor decided to take him off the medication as a result of this healing. His changed attitude changed everything.

YOU ARE LIVING IN TWO WORLDS

You are living in an external and an internal world; yet they both are one. One is visible and the other, invisible (objective and subjective). Your external world enters through your five senses and is shared by everyone. Your internal world of thoughts, feelings, imagination, sensations, beliefs, and reactions is invisible and belongs to you alone.

Ask yourself, "In which world do I live? Do I live in the world that is revealed by my five senses, or in the inner world?" It is in this inner world that you live all the time; this is where you feel and suffer.

Suppose you are invited to a banquet. Everything there that you see, hear, taste, smell, and touch belongs to the external world. All that you think, feel, like, and dislike belongs to your inner world. You actually attend two banquets, which are recorded differently: namely, one the outer, and one the inner. It is your inner world of thought, feeling, and emotion in which you hold your truest existence.

HOW TO TRANSFORM YOURSELF

If you want to grow spiritually, you must transform yourself. How do you do that? To transform yourself, you must begin to change your inner world through the purification of your emotions and by the correct ordering of your mind through right thinking.

Transformation means the changing of one thing into another. There are many well-known transformations of matter. Through a process of chemistry, sugar is changed into alcohol; radium slowly changes into lead. The food you eat is transformed stage by stage into all the substances necessary for your existence.

Your experiences, coming in as impressions, must be similarly transformed. Suppose you see a person whom you love and admire; you receive certain impressions about him or her. Suppose, on the other hand, you meet a person whom you dislike; you also receive impressions, but of a different type. Your spouse or child, sitting on the couch as you read this, is to you what you conceive him or her to be. In other words, impressions are received by your mind.

You can change your impressions of people. To transform your impression is to transform yourself. In order to change your life, change your reactions to life. Do you find yourself reacting in stereotyped ways? If your reactions are negative, you will find yourself sick, morose, morbid, and depressed. Never permit your life to be a series of negative reactions to the impressions that come to you every day.

In order to truly transform yourself, you must reverse every negative thought by claiming that God's love fills your mind and heart. As you make a habit of this, you will become a better person morally, intellectually, and physically. "Who rises from prayer a better man, his prayer is answered" (George Meredith, *The Ordeal of Richard Feverel,* 1859).

You have a panacea for every trouble. *Come unto me, all ye that labour and are heavy laden, and I will give you rest* (Matt. 11:28).

"If in this life we would enjoy the peace of God, we must make our heart a spiritual temple, and whenever we find our thought and feeling wandering away from Him on any occasion, we must bring it back to the contemplation of His Holy Presence" (Brother Lawrence*). "The thoughts of his heart, these are the wealth of a man" (Burmese saying).

---

*From *The Practice of the Presence of God* (1693).

PRAYER FOR CONTROLLING THE EMOTIONS

He that is slow to wrath is of great understanding: but he that is hasty of spirit exalteth folly (Prov. 14:29). I am always poised, serene, and calm. The peace of God floods my mind and my whole being. I practice the Golden Rule and sincerely wish peace and good will to all people.

I know that the love of all things that are good penetrates my mind and casts out all fear. I am now living in the joyous expectancy of the best. My mind is free from all worry and doubt. My words of truth now dissolve every negative thought and emotion within me. I forgive everyone; I open the doorway of my heart to God's Presence. My whole being is flooded with the light and understanding from within.

The petty things of life no longer irritate me. When fear, worry, and doubt knock at my door, faith in goodness, truth, and beauty opens the door, and there is no one there. Oh, God, thou art my God, and there is none else.

THINGS TO WATCH

1. You are here to discipline your thoughts, feelings, and reactions to life.

2. You become emotionally mature as you think, speak, act, and respond from your Divine Center or the God-Self within you.

3. The greatest tyrant is a false idea that controls your mind and holds you in bondage. Immediately supplant it with a new concept of yourself.

4. Love is an emotional attachment; it is outgoing. Pour out love and good will, and you will neutralize all the negative emotions snarled up in your subconscious.

5. You can transmute bad temper into constructive muscular energy by washing windows, playing a game of handball, or digging in your garden.

6. When you get angry, stop and affirm, "I am going to think, speak, and act from the standpoint of wisdom, truth, beauty, and love."

7. You can control your emotional reaction to people by identifying yourself with the Presence of God in each person. Substitute love for hate.

8. Faith in God and all things good casts out fear.

9. Suppressed or repressed emotions bring on all manner of bodily diseases. Become a channel for God and release all your emotions in God-like ways.

10. Substitute a positive, constructive thought for a negative one. The positive emotion of faith and confidence will neutralize and destroy all negative emotions.

11. How do you mentally and emotionally react to events, conditions, and circumstances? It is your reaction that determines your emotion. Think

right, feel right, be right, and do right. No one can disturb you but yourself. Your thought is incipient action. Think God's thoughts, and God's power is with your thoughts of good.

12. You are living in two worlds: the internal world of your thoughts, feelings, imagery, beliefs, and opinions; and the objective world from which impressions are conveyed to you through your five senses. You live in the inner world of your thoughts, feelings, and beliefs. The inner controls the outer.

13. In order to transform yourself, you must purify your emotions through right thinking. Emotion follows thought.

14. To change your life, change your reaction to life. See God in the other, and:

> That thou seest, man,
> Become too thou must;
> God, if thou seest God,
> Dust, if thou seest dust.
> (Brother Angelas)

LAW 11

THE THRILLING LAW OF MARITAL HARMONY

M arriage is the holiest of all earthly unions, and it should be entered into reverently and prayerfully, with full understanding of its sacredness. The sanctity of marriage and the family relation constitute the real cornerstone of our society and civilization.

Marriage, to be complete, must be on a spiritual basis. The contemplation of divine ideals, the study of the laws of life, and a conscious unity in thought, purpose, plan, and action bring about that wedded bliss, that holy union that makes the outer life like the inner: peaceful, joyous, and harmonious.

LOVE UNITES AND FEAR DIVIDES

Christine W. used to live in constant fear that her husband would leave her. "I love him dearly," she said when she told me about her marriage, "and I know he loves me, too. But in some ways we are not very well matched. Harry has no idea of the laws of the conscious and subconscious minds. He sometimes refers to my spiritual interests as head-in-the-clouds stuff. He doesn't mean to be hurtful, it's just that he doesn't understand how much this knowledge means to me."

"Your situation isn't unusual," I told her. "I've run into it many times before. But tell me more about this fear of yours."

"Well, I know it's a negative feeling that I should try to overcome," she replied. "But I never realized how dangerous it could be. I didn't realize I might subconsciously communicate it to Harry. But that's what must have happened. Yesterday morning, at breakfast, he seemed really upset. When I asked what was wrong, he said, 'I think you want to get rid of me. I had a very vivid dream about you last night. You told me, *Get out, I don't want you any more. Don't argue, just go away!*'"

"What did you say?" I asked. "What did you do?"

"I went over and put my arms around him and told him that was all nonsense," she said. "But I could tell I wasn't getting through. What should I do now?"

"Tell him about your fears," I suggested. "Try to make him see that his subconscious mind simply dramatized in a very vivid way the fears and anxieties that were coming from *you*."

Christine followed my advice. After a long talk, her husband understood perfectly. Thereafter, night after night before going to sleep, she countered her fear by picturing her husband as radiant, happy, prosperous, and successful. She radiated the mood of love, peace, and good will to him many times a day, feeling and claiming that he was good, kind, and loving, and that he was a tremendous success.

Her mood of fear changed to a mood of love and peace. She had discovered a great truth: that love brings about an unbroken unity in married life.

THE TRUTH SET HIM FREE

The late Dr. Hester Brunt of Cape Town, South Africa introduced me to a man after one of my lectures in that city. I'll call him Edward A. Dr. Brunt told me that he had served a term in an English prison. After his release, he entered the banking business in Johannesburg, South Africa, married a woman from a prominent family, and was blessed with two wonderful sons. He lived in constant fear, however. He dreaded the possibility that his wife and sons would discover his past, that he would be exposed in the press, and that his wife would thereupon immediately divorce him. He was afraid that this ugly publicity would ruin the future for his two sons. Edward's chronic worry and anxiety caused him to become seriously ill and led to frequent emotional outbursts and tantrums directed at his wife and sons.

I sensed that something was very wrong. According to Dr. Brunt, Edward's doctor could not get him to take the medications he prescribed. I asked Edward, "What is eating you inside?"

He told me about his youthful error and the resulting

time in prison and described his fear of exposure, disgrace, and abandonment. "I'd rather die than face something like that," he told me in an impassioned voice.

I had been thoroughly briefed by Dr. Brunt and by Edward's wife, Joanna.

"There is something you don't know," I said to him. "Your secret is not a secret at all. Your wife, your children, Dr. Brunt, and your superiors at the bank have all known about the mistakes of your earlier life for a long time."

"What!" He turned pale. "I don't understand! How could they? Why did no one ever say anything?"

"Your wife knew even before you were married," I continued. "She never mentioned it because she knew you were a changed man and she did not want to reopen old wounds. As far as she was concerned, your past was a closed book."

Once the truth sank in, that all the people who really mattered in his life knew about his past and loved him for what he was now, Edward astounded his doctor by recovering almost immediately. His suffering and sickness had been due to a distorted mental image. The transformation of his mind resulted in a perfect, harmonious, and peaceful relationship with his wife and sons.

HE DEMANDED A DIVORCE

May S. had been married for thirty years. She and her husband, Mike, had worked side by side to build a business and make it grow, and they had raised three children as well. One day, not long after their youngest child graduated from college, Mike demanded a divorce. He told May he was planning to marry a young woman not much older than their oldest son.

May felt crushed, depressed, and full of foreboding about the future. However, she discovered that she did not have to feel dejected and depressed. She learned how to use the powers of her mind by faithfully practicing the techniques outlined in these pages, and she found an amazing source of strength, inspiration, and courage.

May sold her share of the business and went on a long-planned and long-postponed visit to Europe. She affirmed frequently, "Infinite Intelligence attracts to me a man with whom I harmonize perfectly." While dining at a famous restaurant in southern France, she got into a conversation with the man at the next table, a diplomat who had taken early retirement. As they continued to talk, she realized that he was ideal for her. He was clearly arriving at a similar realization about her.

A few weeks later, May and her diplomat were married in Paris. All three of her children flew over from the United States for the ceremony. May found that her divorce had been a bridge that led her into a richer, grander, nobler, and more God-like life. She had learned to meet the challenge of despair and loneliness with confidence and trust in the infinite wisdom of her subconscious mind.

MARRIED FIVE TIMES

Verona G., a young woman of 28, consulted me. "Would you believe I've been married five times!" she declared. "And each husband has been worse than the one before!"

She was bitter and resentful as she described each of her marriages, beginning with the boy she wed right out of high school.

"You know," I said, "this is not accidental. Your resentment and hostility becomes magnified in your subconscious mind and leads you to attract and be attracted by men who have an affinity to those negative feelings. That is the reason each of your partners has seemed worse than the one before. It is the operation of the law of attraction. Like draws like. Birds of a feather really do flock together."

Verona was silent for a long while. Then she said, "I can see how I've fallen into a terrible trap. But how do I get out of it?"

"The key is forgiveness," I replied. "You must set yourself and your former husbands free. You must replace your attitude of resentment with one of love and peace. If you can sincerely affirm, 'I release you and let you go, wishing for you health, wealth, love, happiness, peace, and joy,' you will find your whole understanding of love and marriage changed to a more spiritual basis."

Verona accepted my suggestion. She realized that her previous attitudes and motives for marriage were all wrong. She began to pray three or four times daily as follows:

I know that I am one with God now. In Him I live, move, and have my being. God is life; this life is the life of all men and women. We are all sons and daughters of the one Father. I know and believe that there is a man waiting to love and cherish me. I know I can contribute to his happiness and peace. He loves my ideals, and I love his ideals. He does not want to make me over; neither do I want to make him over. There are mutual love, freedom, and respect.

There is one mind; I know him now in this mind. I now unite with the qualities and attributes that I admire and want expressed by my husband. I am one with them in my mind. We know and love each other in Divine Mind. I see the God in him; he sees the God in me. Having met him within, I must meet him in the without, for this is the law of my own mind.

These words go forth and accomplish whereunto they are sent. I know it is now done, finished, and accomplished in God. Thank you, Father.

A few weeks later Verona needed to have a wisdom tooth removed. A beautiful friendship developed with the dentist. Eventually he proposed marriage—as she said, "right out of the blue"—and she added, "I knew intuitively he was the man about whom I had prayed. It was a case of love at first sight." I had the gratification of performing their marriage ceremony, and I could see it was a real spiritual union of two people seeking their way back to the heart of God.

HOW HE FOUND HIS IDEAL

I was leading a series of services in Rochester, New York when Gilbert M. came to me urgently for help. "I've been going with a certain woman for almost three years," he told me. "I've asked her more than once to marry me. The last time was just last month. She always said 'Maybe later.' Last night she told me she didn't want to see me any more. I don't know why, all I know is that I can't live without her. I'm desperate!"

"I can see that, and I sympathize with the pain you are feeling," I said. "If your goal is a happy, harmonious marriage, you must pray for it. Prayers *are* answered, you know!"

At my suggestion, he began to pray every morning and every night for a wife, in the following manner:

God is one and indivisible. In Him we live, move, and have our being. I know and believe that God indwells every person; I am one with God and with all people. I now attract the right woman who is in complete accord with me. This is a spiritual union, because it is the spirit of God functioning through the personality of someone with whom I blend perfectly. I know I can give to this woman love, light, and truth. I know I can make this woman's life full, complete, and wonderful.

I now decree that she possesses the following qualities and attributes: She is spiritual, loyal, faithful, and true. She is harmonious, peaceful, and happy. We are irresistibly attracted to each other. Only that which belongs to love, truth, and wholeness can enter my experience. I accept my ideal companion now.

Gilbert continued mentally and emotionally to unite with these truths every night and morning. Soon he subjectively absorbed them and impressed them upon his subconscious mind, which is after all a manifestation of the universal mind. After a few weeks, he met a woman who had recently joined the division of the company where he worked. He fell in love with her and she with him. Later in the year, they were married.

What about the woman Gilbert was so sure he could

not live without? He later discovered that, for much of the time they had been going together, she had also been involved with another man, whom she eventually married!

THAT'S THE MAN I WANT

Rose L., a legal secretary in London, said to me during an interview, "I am in love with my boss. George is married and has four children, but I don't care. I've set my heart on him, and I will get him whatever it takes. As for his wife, that's her lookout, isn't it?"

Rose seemed perfectly willing to break up a home in order to gain her point. However, I explained to her that what she really wanted was not this married man. Her deepest desire was to have what she believed he and his wife had—a relationship in which each partner loved, cherished, and admired the other. "There is an ideal mate for you," I assured her, "one who is searching for you as hard as you search for him, and who will come to you without the encumbrance of an ongoing relationship with someone else. You can attract that mate to you, if you choose to."

"Why should I?" she demanded. "George is right there already. That's the man I want!"

"You may succeed in possessing this man," I replied. "You may manage to bend him to your will. But you have no idea of the problems and difficulties you will be making for yourself. You will impregnate your subconscious mind with a sense of limitation and guilt. You know the commandment: *Thou shalt not covet thy neighbour's wife* (Ex. 20:17). And the even greater commandment, *Whatsoever ye would that men should do to you, do ye even so to them* (Matt. 7:12). These words give the entire law of a happy and successful life. In selfishness and greed, this is forgotten."

"Yes, but—," Rose started to say. She stopped, confused.

I pressed the point. "What would you like George's children to think of you? How do you want them to feel about you? Wouldn't you like them to see you as a noble, gentle, dignified lady who is honest, sincere, and upright? Apply this principle and decide if you still want to tear their family apart."

Rose suddenly saw the truth of what she was proposing to do and broke into sobs. Once she was quiet again, she agreed that she would want to attract an ideal companion without causing grief or pain to anyone else. She prayed by affirming: "I am now attracting a wonderful man who harmonizes with me spiritually, mentally, and physically. He comes to me without encumbrances and in divine order."

Shortly thereafter, Rose began to attend the London Truth Forum, in London's Caxton Hall, at my suggestion. At one of these meetings, she met a young chemist who turned out to be the man she *really* wanted. She discovered in this way that there is a law of mind that will bring to pass whatever she would accept as true.

LOVE IS A ONENESS

Why do people cheat on their partners? If you have true love and respect for your mate, you do not want anyone else. Once someone has found a true, spiritual ideal in marriage, he or she has no desire for someone different. Love is a oneness; it is not a duality or a multiplicity.

Those who embrace promiscuity are "marrying" (mentally and emotionally uniting with) many negative concepts, such as frustration, resentment, and cynicism. Those who have found love with a mate have found fullness of life. If they play around outside of the relationship, therefore, it must be that they are frustrated and have never really experienced ideal love, or a feeling of oneness. To their inferiority complex they add, undoubtedly, a guilt complex.

Inevitably, the people they meet are vacillating, neurotic, and confused; they are seeing and hearing their own inner vibrations. The temporary partners they find are just as frustrated and unstable as themselves. Birds of a feather flock together. Like begets like.

AVOID A DEAD-END STREET

Vickie Y. was brought to meet me by her worried younger sister. Vickie, a systems analyst in her early thirties, was quite open about the fact that she was deeply involved with someone she worked with, a married man.

"We've been seeing each other for four years," she told me. "I'm very attached to him, and I think he is to me, too. In the beginning I thought he would leave his wife and marry me, but now . . . I don't know. It doesn't look that way, does it?"

"It certainly doesn't," I agreed, "and from his standpoint, why should he? He has his wife, his home, *and you*. Why should he settle for less than what he has already?"

"You make it sound so crass!" Vickie said with a shudder. "Doesn't affection count for anything?"

"True affection is golden," I said. "But would true affection keep you in the position you are in now? What you're doing happens all the time, but it usually ends in a blind alley or a dead-end street. What you really want, I am sure, is a home, a stable partnership, the respect and affection of neighbors, friends, and family. Your present entanglement does not give you any of that. Instead, it keeps you from achieving them."

As we talked, Vickie came to see that the answer to her problem was prayer. She immediately broke off the relationship with her married coworker and began to practice the prayer to attract the ideal partner that was quoted earlier in this chapter.

Two months later, Vickie began dating a man her sister introduced her to. As a result, she is now happily married. She is genuinely grateful for having discovered the inner powers of her mind.

SHOULD I GET A DIVORCE?

How often it happens that someone comes to me and asks, "Should I get a divorce?" I tell them there is no one answer. This is an individual problem. It cannot be generalized. In some cases divorce is not the solution, any more than marriage is necessarily the solution for someone who is chronically lonely.

Divorce may be right for one person and wrong for another. In some cases, there never was a real marriage in the first place. Just because a man and woman have a marriage certificate and live in a house together, it does not follow that it is a real home. It may instead be a place of discord and hatred. When children are present and the parents refuse to radiate love, peace, and good will to each other, it is better to dissolve the union than to have the mood of hatred warp the minds of the youngsters. Many times a child's life and mind are permanently affected by the mood of the parents, leading to neurosis, delinquency, and crime. It is far better for children to live with one parent who loves them than to live with two who hate each other and fight all the time.

Where there is no love, freedom, or respect between husband and wife, such a marriage is a farce, a sham, and a masquerade, because God (Love) has not joined them together. God is Love, and the heart is the chamber of God's Presence; when two hearts are joined together in mutual love, that is a real marriage because Love has joined them together.

GET A NEW ESTIMATE OF YOURSELF

We demote ourselves when we focus on our insufficiency and lack. We transmit our fears to our partners, who cannot help but react in kind. They no longer see us in the way they once did, because we no longer see ourselves as we once did. Each partner, then, comes to see the other as that other sees himself or herself. It cannot be otherwise.

Those who feel themselves to be dignified command respect. Those who face the daily trials of life with a predominant mood of success and happiness knit together all the members of their household. They become a cementing and stabilizing influence. Harmony and peace reign supreme in the household. Your dominant conviction makes others see what you see.

BECOMING A SUCCESSFUL HUSBAND OR WIFE

When you married your husband or wife, you must have admired certain of his or her characteristics, virtues, and qualities. Identify with the good qualities and exalt them. Cease being a scavenger by dwelling on the shortcomings of each other. Make a list of his or her good points, and give your attention and devotion to them. As you do this, your marriage will grow more blessed and beautiful through the years.

THE BIBLICAL FORMULA

What therefore God hath joined together, let not man put asunder (Matt. 19:6). This biblical formula reveals to you that in order for a marriage to be real, it must first be spiritual; it must be of the heart. If both your hearts are moved by love, sincerity, and honesty, then that is God joining both of you together; truly, it is the marriage made in heaven, which means harmony and understanding. You know and feel that the action of your heart is love, and God is Love.

God is not present in *all* marriages. Perhaps there were ulterior motives in the union. If a man marries a woman for money, for position, or to satisfy his ego, that marriage is false; it is a lie. If a woman marries a man for security, wealth, position, a thrill, or to get even with someone else, such a marriage is not of God; for God, or the Truth, was not present. Such marriages are not real because they are not based on love. Honesty, integrity, and respect are born of love.

Where there is a real, true, heavenly marriage—a union of hearts, minds, and bodies—there can be no divorce. Neither do they seek divorce, for it is a spiritual union. It is a union of two hearts. They are united in love. *What therefore God hath joined together, let not man put asunder* (Matt. 19:6).

MARRIAGE PRAYER
FOR HUSBAND AND WIFE

We are gathered together in the Presence of God. There is but One God, One Life, One Law, One Mind, and One Father— our Father. We are united in love, harmony, and peace. I rejoice in the peace, happiness, and success of my mate. God is guiding each one of us at all times. We speak to each other from the standpoint of the Divine Center within us. Our words to each other are as a honeycomb, sweet to the ear and pleasant to the bones. We identify with the good qualities of each other and constantly exalt them.

The Love of God flows through us to all in our household and to all people everywhere. We believe and know that the Omnipresent Power and Intelligence of the Infinite One move through each one of us and all members of our household, and that we are positively, definitely, physically, and mentally healed. We know that divine right action is taking place in every cell, organ, tissue, and function of each one of us, manifesting as peace, harmony, and health.

We believe that divine guidance is now being experienced by everyone in this household. God, the Great Counselor, leads each one of us to ways of pleasantness and paths of peace.

The words we speak now shall accomplish what we please and prosper whereunto they are sent. We rejoice now and enter into the mood of thankfulness, knowing that our prayer of faith is fulfilled.

STEP THIS WAY TO A HAPPY MARRIAGE

1. Marriage is the holiest of all earthly unions. It should be entered into reverently, peacefully, and with a deep understanding of its sacredness.

2. A spouse's constant fear can be communicated to the subconscious of the other spouse and cause endless trouble.

3. The past is dead. The only thing that matters is the present moment. Change your present thought and keep it changed, and you change your destiny. Suffering is due to ignorance and distorted mental pictures.

4. Meet the challenge of loneliness and despair with confidence and trust in the infinite wisdom of your subconscious mind.

5. You attract the affinities of your dominant subconscious mood. Forgive yourself and everybody else, and then pray for a divine companion by building into your mentality the qualities you admire in a mate.

6. Infinite Intelligence will attract to you the ideal husband or wife if you pray sincerely and trust your deeper mind to bring your request to pass.

7. You must never covet another person's wife or husband. Claim what you want, believe that Life will give it to you, and you shall have it.

8. Love is oneness, and if you are really in love with your husband or wife, you could not want another.

9. Many husbands and wives living together are divorced from love, kindness, peace, harmony, good will, and understanding. Such a marriage is a farce, a sham, and a masquerade. It is better to break up such a lie than to continue living the lie.

10. We demote ourselves by feeling lack and inferiority, and our partners usually react accordingly.

11. Identify with the good qualities and characteristics of your mate, and your marriage will grow more blessed through the years.

12. *What therefore God* [Love] *hath joined together, let not man put asunder* (Matt. 19:6). When love unites two hearts together, there is no divorce, for Love is the knot that binds man and woman in the endless course of life, now and forevermore.

LAW 12

THE GLORIOUS LAW OF PEACE OF MIND

Millions of people throughout the world are literally sick from worrying. People who worry always expect things to go wrong. Their worry is primarily due to a lack of faith in God. They brood or worry over a great many things that may never happen. They will tell you all the reasons why something bad could happen, and not one reason why something good should or could happen. This constant worry debilitates their entire system, resulting in physical and mental disorders.

HE WORRIED ABOUT WHAT HAD NOT HAPPENED

At a meeting of a community organization, I fell into conversation with a local pharmacist, Fred B. When I asked him how things were going, he said, "Terrible. I am frankly worried sick. I can't sleep nights. I'm afraid I'll lose the drugstore, and everything I've saved for retirement, too."

"Is business that bad?" I asked, astonished. "I had the impression things are booming these days."

"I suppose you could say that," Fred replied. "It's true, my receipts are up substantially, but it can't last. You know what they say: Every boom ends in a bust."

"I have to say, I never heard that before," I told him. "What exactly is the problem with your business, Fred? Did you borrow a lot to expand? Did you lose one of your important accounts?"

"No, nothing like that," he admitted. "Nothing in particular. I suppose if you went by my books, you'd say everything is fine. But I worry all the time about what's going to happen down the road. I'm sure I'm going to end my days a bankrupt failure, depending on my kids to support me. It ties my stomach in knots, just talking like this." He pulled a package of antacids from his pocket and swallowed one.

Fred's constant negative thinking was robbing him of vitality, enthusiasm, and energy. Even more ominous, he was making himself weaker and less able to meet any challenges that might come along. Moreover, the negative perspective he was impressing upon his subconscious mind practically guaranteed that some such challenge or difficulty would erupt.

I explained to him that if he continued worrying, he would attract exactly the conditions upon which he was mentally dwelling. The only thing really wrong with him was a false belief in his mind. He had forgotten, or never learned, that he could personally control his thoughts and his life. I gave him the following prayer for his business:

> My business is God's business. God is my partner in all of my affairs. God is prospering my business in a wonderful way. I claim that all those working with me in my store are spiritual links in its growth, welfare, and prosperity; I know this, I believe it, and I rejoice in their success and happiness. I solve all my problems by trusting the infinite intelligence within my subconscious mind to reveal to me the answer.
>
> I rest in security and peace. I am surrounded by peace, love, and harmony. I know that all my business relationships with people are in accord with the law of harmony. Infinite Intelligence reveals to me better ways in which I can serve humanity. I know that God indwells all of my customers and clients. I work harmoniously with others to the end that happiness, prosperity, and peace reign supreme. Whenever any worry thoughts come to my mind, I will immediately affirm, *I will fear no evil: for thou art with me* (Ps. 23:4).

Fred began to set aside ten or fifteen minutes every morning, afternoon, and evening for the purpose of reiterating these truths. He realized that through their frequent habitation of his mind, he would be reconditioned to constructive thinking. When morbid thoughts came to his mind, he would immediately affirm, "God is with me." He later said to me that on one day, he must have said "God is with me" about a thousand times.

Gradually the neurotic thought pattern of chronic worry that he had complained of in the beginning, and that had been repeating itself with monotonous regularity, was completely dissipated, and he rejoiced in his freedom in God.

SHE HEALED HER
ANXIETY NEUROSIS

I received a letter from a woman named Agatha R., from Montana, in which she wrote, "My husband sits around all day and does nothing but drink beer. He won't work, and he whines all the time. He worries me terribly, and my doctor says that I'm getting an anxiety disorder. On top of that, I suffer from asthma, skin trouble, and high blood pressure. My husband is killing me."

I wrote back and told her that today it is well known in psychological and medical circles that many skin disorders, asthma, allergies, cardiac disorders, and diabetes, as well as a host of other illnesses, are worsened by chronic worry, which is another name for her anxiety disorder. I gave her a spiritual prescription. I suggested that several times a day, she was to bless her husband as follows:

My husband is God's man. He is divinely active, divinely prospered, peaceful, happy, and joyous. He is expressing himself fully and is in his true place; he receives a marvelous income. Sobriety and peace of mind reign supreme in his life. I now picture him coming home every night and telling me how happy he is in his new job, and I leave it all to God to fulfill.

I enclosed a second prescription that Agatha was to take mentally and emotionally six or seven times a day until her subconscious absorbed it. She was to picture her doctor telling her that she was whole and perfect, and to pray in these words:

The gifts of God are mine. I use every moment of this day to glorify God. God's harmony, peace, and abundance are mine. Divine love flowing from me blesses all who come into my atmosphere. God's love is healing me now. I fear no evil, for God is with me. I am always surrounded by the sacred circle of God's love and power. I claim, feel, know, and believe definitely and positively that the spell of God's love and eternal watchfulness guides, heals, and takes care of all members of my family and loved ones.

I forgive everyone, and I sincerely radiate God's love, peace, and good will to all men everywhere. At the center of my being is peace; this is the peace of God. In this stillness I feel His strength and guidance and the love of His Holy Presence. I am divinely guided in all my ways. I am a clear channel for God's love, light, truth, and beauty. I feel His river of peace flowing through me. I know that all of my problems are dissolved in the Mind of God. God's ways are my ways. The words I have spoken accomplish that whereunto they are sent. I rejoice and give thanks, realizing that my prayers are answered. It is so.

Not long afterward, I received a telephone call from Agatha. "Your prayers worked wonders!" she exclaimed. "I have been saying the prayers as you suggested, and I have been holding a picture of my husband in my mind. The result was, he went out and got a good, well-paying job. Not only that, he's sober. All the itchy blotches on my skin have cleared up, and on my last visit to my doctor, my blood pressure was normal. I don't have to take asthma medicine any more."

This woman's accumulated negative thoughts and mental pictures were the cause of her chronic worry. As she identified mentally and emotionally with the truths given her, they began to sink into her mind. She also painted pictures of health and vitality for herself and of achievement and accomplishment for her husband. These mental images were etched on her deeper mind, and her subconscious brought them all to fruition.

HIS WORRY WAS NOT CAUSED BY HIS PROBLEM

David W. was a high-level executive with a growing corporation. He came to me because he was terribly worried. The CEO of the company was retiring and David was the obvious candidate to succeed him. He was convinced that something would happen before the next board meeting to keep him from being given the position he had been working toward for so long. He added that the constant worry and anxiety were about to give him a nervous breakdown.

In talking to David, I discovered that he had been worrying about something or other for most of his life. I remarked that while he thought his worry was due to the possibility that he would not be chosen, it seemed to me that that was simply the focus of it at this moment. He did not agree. He became quite vehement about it. Accordingly, I told him to picture himself as CEO and to visualize his associates congratulating him on his promotion. He faithfully followed these instructions, and he was duly installed as CEO at the next board meeting.

About a month later, David came to see me again. He was still worrying, and his doctor had said that his blood pressure was dangerously high. I reminded him that he had previously attributed his worry to the thought that he might not be made head of his company. Now that he *was* head, why hadn't he stopped worrying?

"It's a lot of things," he said. "The buck stops at my desk. What if I can't live up to the board's expectations? Not to mention those people on Wall Street. They're watching every move, and the first time we hit a bump, our stock valuation may go south, and my job with it. I could be unemployed three weeks from now!"

"I think you'd be wise to look inside yourself," I said. "It seems to me that that is where your worries really come from. Your real problem is not the price of your company's stock. It is the fact that you do not make a habit of prayer and have no real contact with Infinite Power from which you could draw strength and security. I know you believe you are cursed with these worries by outside circumstances. In reality, however, you alone are their creator, and you alone can overcome them."

"Tell me how," David demanded. "I'll do anything!"

I suggested that every morning, first thing, he use the following prayer:

I know that the answer to my problem lies in the God-Self within me. I now become quiet, still, and relaxed. I am at peace. I know God speaks in peace and not in confusion. I am now in tune with the Infinite; I know and believe implicitly that Infinite Intelligence is revealing to me the perfect answer. I think about the solution to my problems. I now live in the mood I would have were my problem solved. I truly live in this abiding faith and trust, which is the mood of the solution; this is the spirit of God moving within me. This Spirit is Omnipotent; it is manifesting itself and my whole being rejoices in the solution; I am glad. I live in this feeling and I give thanks.

I know that God has the answer, for with God all things are possible. God is the Living Spirit Almighty within me; He is the Source of all wisdom and illumination.

The indicator of the presence of God within me is a sense of peace and poise. I now cease all sense of strain and struggle; I trust the God-Power implicitly. I know that all the wisdom and power I need to live a glorious and successful life are within me. I relax my entire body; my faith is in His wisdom; I go free. I claim and feel the peace of God flooding my mind, my heart, and my whole being. I know that the quiet mind gets its problems solved. I now turn my request over to the God-Presence, knowing it has an answer. I am at peace.

David repeated this prayer three times each morning, knowing that through repetition these truths would sink into his subconscious and establish a healing, wholesome habit of constructive thinking. He also realized that he was now anchored to the God-Power within him in which he lived, moved, and had his being. His sense of union with God gave him confidence to overcome anything about which he had mistakenly worried. Through this shift in his mental attitude, he became a balanced man.

HOW SHE GOT OFF
THE MERRY-GO-ROUND

Virginia L. came to see me because she was preoccupied with worry about her ten-year-old son, Ricky. "Every day when I see him off to school, I'm convinced he'll be run over or kidnapped. And what about disease? There are so many terrible diseases going around these days. I just can't seem to stop worrying."

"Wouldn't it be much more interesting, fascinating, absorbing, and thrilling to bless your son, instead of throwing mental bricks at him all day long?" I asked. I suggested that she open her mind, let in the Higher Power, and realize that God loves her son, that He watches over him, that His Overshadowing Presence protects the child at all times, and that God's love surrounds him, enfolds him, and enwraps him.

As Virginia practiced blessing her son, she cast out all her gloom of worry and misery. She made a habit of prayer—and prayer is a habit.

This woman's obsessive worry, fretfulness, and morbid thoughts about her son were due ultimately to laziness and indifference. She allowed these destructive pictures to influence her thoughts and emotions. You can heal yourself as she did, by following the injunction of the Psalmist: *I will lift up mine eyes unto the hills, from whence cometh my help* (Ps. 121:1). Do this regularly and you will be released from the vexation of worry.

YOU DON'T WANT IT

When you worry, you are focusing your mental energies and directing your mind toward what you *don't* want. In this way, you create conditions, experiences, and events that disturb you. Worry means that you are using your mind negatively and destructively.

HOW WORRY AFFECTS ALL GLANDS AND ORGANS OF OUR BODIES

Dr. Hans Selye of the University of Montreal was one of the first scientists to demonstrate the destructive effects of worry, fear, and anxiety on the immune system, the general defense system of the body.

When you are under mental stress, your adrenal glands try to correct the situation. They increase the output of important hormones. If the stress continues over a period of weeks, however, these vital glands become exhausted. Eventually, resistance breaks down, and you are at risk for illness and even death. Stress is an adaptive reaction in the short run, but over time it compromises your health and well-being. It is one thing to find yourself having to run away from a lion or wrestle an alligator. Mobilizing all the body's resources makes very good sense in those situations. But if the body stays mobilized for a longer period, it is like a country that has gone onto a war alert: The ordinary business of life gets shortchanged.

Dr. Selye's work demonstrated that the human defense system can effectively fight only one thing at a time. In response to a mental tension caused by pain from a broken limb, for instance, it is set into action and quickly organizes a hundred specialized activities, in addition to its general work, to repair the fracture. But if in the middle of this repair work another stress is introduced—one caused by fear, let us say—we quickly succumb either to the first injury or to shock resulting from the second stress, or the broken limb simply does not mend properly. In the case of other diseases, healing is suspended and the diseases become chronic. Thus, if our general defense system is mobilized by mental tensions of a nonphysical origin, our resistance to the extra stresses imposed by such things as pneumonia, influenza, and other infectious or systemic diseases is decreased proportionally.

HE RAISED HIS SIGHTS

A young intern consistently worried about his future; he was a nervous wreck. However, he learned to paint a picture of himself as filling a staff position in a big hospital and being singled out for his skill and knowledge in a magazine article about the medical profession.

He kept this mental picture before him at all times. He attended to it and devoted himself to this visualization. Whenever he found himself starting to worry, he purposefully turned his attention to the image of his realized goals. As the weeks passed by, a higher power moved on his behalf, honoring his dreams and making them all real. The chief surgeon, impressed by the intern's dexterity and knowledge, invited him to be his assistant. Later, that same surgeon mentioned the intern's name to a writer as one of the most promising young doctors at the hospital. The intern was interviewed, then followed for a day, and his portrait illustrated the resulting article.

This is the way the habit of worry is changed. This is the way the old person becomes a new person in God. *Cast thy burden upon the Lord, and he shall sustain thee* (Ps. 55:22).

YOU CAN OVERCOME WORRY

Do not spend time looking at your troubles or problems; cease all negative thinking. Your mind cannot function harmoniously when it is tense. It relieves the strain to do something soothing and pleasant when you are presented with a problem. Do not *fight* a problem; *overcome* it.

To release pressure, take a drive, go for a walk, play solitaire, or read a favorite chapter of the Bible, such as the eleventh chapter of Hebrews or chapter thirteen of 1 Corinthians. Or, read the Forty-sixth Psalm; read it over carefully and quietly several times. An inner calm will steal over you, and you will become poised and peaceful.

STEPS IN PRAYER
FOR OVERCOMING WORRY

The First Step

Every morning when you awaken, turn to God in prayer and know that God is your loving Father. Relax your body; then have a dialogue with God, which is your Higher Self. Become as a little child; this means that you trust the God-Presence completely and you know that God is healing you now.

The Second Step

Affirm lovingly: "Thank you, Father, for this wonderful day. It is God's day; it is filled with joy, peace, happiness, and success for me. I look forward with a happy expectancy to this day. The wisdom and inspiration of God will govern me during the entire day. God is my partner; everything I do will turn out in a wonderful way. I believe that God is guiding me, and His love fills my soul."

The Third Step

Claim boldly: "I am full of confidence in the goodness of God. I know that He watches over me at all times. I let go; I am poised, serene, and calm. I know that it is God in action in all phases of my life, and divine law and order reign supreme."

Make a habit of following these three steps to prayer. When worry thoughts come to your mind, substitute any of the spiritual thoughts from these three steps. Gradually your mind will be conditioned to peace.

POWER-POINTERS

1. When you worry, you brood over a great many things that will never happen, and you deplete yourself of vitality, enthusiasm, and energy.

2. When you worry, you are anxious not about what *has* happened, but about what *might* happen. Change your present mode of thought and you will change your future. Your future is your present thought made manifest.

3. If you sustain the worry habit, you may attract what you are worrying about.

4. When morbid, negative thoughts come to your mind, overcome them by affirming: "God is with me." This destroys the negative thought.

5. If you are worried about people close to you, mentally picture them as you would wish to see them. Frequent habitation of your mind with this picture will work miracles.

6. Chronic worriers are not worried about the problem they say they are worried about. The basic reason is a deep sense of insecurity, because they have not joined themselves with God.

7. Don't worry about your child in school. Realize the Presence of God where your child is, and mentally envelop the child with God's love, peace, and joy. Know that the whole armor of God enfolds your child, and that he or she will always be protected from all harm.

8. When you worry, you are really praying for what you don't want.

9. Unite with a Higher Power and let the Almighty move through your new constructive pattern of thought and imagery; then the Light of God will dispel all gloom, worry, and despair. Let in the sunshine of His love.

LAW 13

THE REPLENISHING LAW OF AUTOMATIC PROSPERITY

People constantly ask me, "How can I get ahead in life, improve my circumstances, earn a higher salary, buy a new car and a new home, send my kids through college, and have the money I need in order to do what I have to do when I want to do it?"

The answer to all of these questions comes through learning to use the laws of your own mind: the law of cause and effect, the law of increase, and the law of attraction. These laws of your mind work with the same precision and exactitude as do the laws of physics, chemistry, and mathematics, and as definitely as the law of gravitation. The law of prosperity is beautifully expressed by the Psalmist who says, *His delight is in the law of the Lord; and in his law doth he meditate day and night* (Ps. 1:2).

Achieving prosperity means to increase our capacities and abilities along all lines and in every direction so that we release our inner powers. The promotion, the money, and the contacts you wish to make are the images or likenesses, as well as the physical forms of the states of mind that produce them.

HOW A BROKER PROSPERED

I have known Randolph T., a Los Angeles stockbroker, for many years. He attributes his large clientele and success in making money for them to his practice of a mental, imaginary conversation. Every morning before he goes to his office, he visualizes an interchange with a banker friend who is a celebrated investor. This multimillionaire friend congratulates Randolph on his wise and sound judgment and compliments him on steering his clients toward the right stocks. Randolph dramatizes this imaginary conversation and he psychologically fixes the impression on his subconscious.

This broker's imaginary conversations agree with his aim to make sound investments for himself and his clients. He told me that his main purpose in his business life is to make money for others and to see them prosper financially through his wise counsel. In making money for others, he has also prospered beyond his fondest dreams. It is quite evident that he is using the laws of mind constructively and that his delight is in the law of the Lord.

HIS SUBCONSCIOUS
PAID HIS MORTGAGE

Vernon K. came to me in a panic. "I'm in a terrible fix," he said. "I've been buying speculative stocks on margin. For a couple of years, I made out like a bandit. Everything I bought went up and up and up. So I borrowed on the shares and bought more. At one point, my worth on paper was well over a million dollars. I thought I was really hot stuff."

"I think I can guess what happened next," I said.

"I wouldn't be surprised," Vernon replied. "I discovered the law of gravity, that's what. 'What goes up must come down.' Some of my favorite stocks lost thirty or forty percent of their value in just a few days. So I did what I always do, buy on the dips. With borrowed money, I might add. But the dips got deeper. Pretty soon my broker was on my case with margin calls. I had to borrow against my house and car to stay in the game."

"A very dangerous game, I must point out," I said.

"You're telling me!" Vernon replied, rolling his eyes. "I'll cut to the chase. If I don't come up with another $30,000 by Monday morning, my broker will sell me out. I'll lose everything I have and still be in debt over my ears. You're my last resort, my only hope. Can you do anything?"

"No," I said. Before he could react to this, I quickly added, "but you can. If you use your subconscious mind in the right way, it will provide you with the money you need."

"How? Please, tell me," he begged.

"You're not to wonder how, when, or where," I replied. "Don't wonder about the source. The subconscious has ways you know not of. Its ways are past finding out."

At my suggestion, that night Vernon imagined himself walking into his broker's office and handing him the necessary sum. He visualized the broker saying, "You're in the clear now. I'm glad. I think your portfolio's hit bottom and will start to go up again now."

Vernon focused all his energies on this mental picture. He made it seem real and natural. The more earnestly he engaged his mind in the imaginary drama, the more effectively the imaginary act was deposited in the bank of his subconscious. He made it so real and true that it had to take place physically.

A few days later, Vernon told me the sequel to this story. That same night, he had a vivid dream of a horse taking first place in a race at the Hollywood Race Track. He knew, in his dream, that the horse was a 60-to-1 long shot. He then dreamed that the cashier at the race track counted out $30,000 and said, "Congratulations on your win, sir." Immediately afterward, he woke up with every detail of the dream sharp in his mind. He awakened his wife and told her of his dream. She said, "I have five hundred-dollar bills tucked away for a rainy day. Now, those bills will rain blessings from Heaven for us. Go to the track and put them on the horse!"

Vernon's horse came in at 60 to 1, just as he had seen in his dream. As the race track cashier was paying him off, he said the exact words Vernon had heard in his dream. He went straight from the track to his broker's office and paid off the margin debt, in the same way that he had previously subjectively visualized so vividly and earnestly.

I the Lord will make myself known unto him in a vision, and will speak unto him in a dream (Num. 12:6).

THE MAGIC OF INCREASE

"I'm an unemployed Web site designer," Valerie A. wrote to me. "I'm also the single mother of a four-year-old. The bills are piling up, and I'm just a few weeks from running through my benefits. What do I do if my child gets sick? What shall I do?"

My response was to suggest that Valerie begin to give thanks for God's bountiful supply. Several times a day, she relaxed her body in an armchair and entered into a drowsy, sleepy state, or a state akin to sleep. She condensed the ideas of her needs into these wonderful magic-working words of increase: "God multiplies my good exceedingly." She understood that whatever she gave attention to, her subconscious would magnify and multiply a hundredfold. The significance of these words to her meant the realization of all of her desires, including being able to pay all her bills; finding a new, well-paying position in her field; and having enough money to be able to stop worrying.

During her periods of prayer, she did not permit her mind to wander; she focused and concentrated her attention on the meaning of the words, "God multiplies my good exceedingly." She repeated this phrase over and over again until it had the feeling of reality.

The idea of using a simple phrase in this way is based upon a knowledge of the laws of mind. When you restrict your attention to one simple phrase, your mind is prevented from wandering. Ideas are conveyed to the subconscious by repetition, faith, and expectancy.

Valerie's disciplined visualization brought astounding results. Three weeks later, she received a call from an attorney. A company she had worked for two years earlier owned the patents on a process that had just been found to be very valuable. The shares of stock she had written off as worthless were now valued at almost $50,000. She sold the stock, paid off all her debts, and used some of the balance to set up a consulting firm with one of the people from her last job. She later told me that she is supremely happy.

The ways of the subconscious truly are past finding out. Your subconscious multiplies thirtyfold, sixtyfold, and hundredfold. This is the magic of increase.

"THANK YOU" OPENS THE WAY TO PROSPERITY

It is amazing how the thankful attitude improves every department of your life, your health and happiness as well as your prosperity.

A real estate broker I know named Rick W. proved this in a wonderful way. He had been having a great deal of difficulty selling homes and properties that were listed with him. He was frustrated and unhappy. Convinced of the prosperity-power of the grateful heart, however, he began to pray every night, affirming as follows: "Father, I thank thee that thou hast heard me, and I know that thou hearest me always." Then, just prior to sleep, he condensed the phrase to two words: "Thank you." He repeated them over and over again, as a lullaby; he continued to speak these two words silently until he fell asleep.

One morning a woman came into Rick's office whose face he was sure he recognized. He prided himself on his memory for names and faces, but when she introduced herself, the name meant nothing at all to him. At that moment, he realized that he had seen her in a dream a night or two earlier. While he was still pondering this amazing fact, she told him that she represented a consortium that was actively investing in rental properties. By the end of the day, Rick had sold her group more properties than he had sold over the previous month.

Since that breakthrough, Rick has made a habit of feelingly repeating the words "Thank you" every night until he falls asleep. His health has improved remarkably, his wealth is growing, and often, in his dreams, he has a preview of the sale of certain properties that later comes true.

You can follow Rick's example. Silently decree morning and night that God is prospering you in mind, body, and affairs. Feel the reality of it, and you will never want for anything. Repeat over and over again as a lullaby, "Thank you, Father," as you prepare for sleep. This means that you are thanking your Higher Self for abundance, health, wealth, and harmony. It may also happen that the Lord (your subconscious mind) may answer you in a vision and speak to you in a dream.

LIFE IS ADDITION

Martin P., a friend of mine in the construction trade, has a favorite saying: "All I ever do is add. I never subtract." What he means is that prosperity is a plus sign. Add to your growth, wealth, power, knowledge, faith, and wisdom.

Martin adds to his life by meditating on success, harmony, guidance, right action, and the law of opulence. He imagines and feels himself successful and prosperous, and his subconscious mind responds to his habitual thinking.

Your subconscious always magnifies. As the Bible says, *Thou shalt also decree a thing, and it shall be established unto thee* (Job 22:28).

SHE BEGAN TO SELL AGAIN

Betty W. recently finished her third year with a major insurance company. She is as committed as ever to a career in the field, but she finds the day-to-day conditions harder and harder to handle. As she said when she described her problem to me, "I know I'm doing my clients a service when I get them to check their insurance coverage. It's not just a question of selling them another policy. But if I make a hundred calls, I'm lucky if five are reasonably receptive and one of those actually gives me business. It's hard to live with that kind of discouragement."

I arranged for Betty to have a session with me once a week. At these sessions I had her still her mind, relax, and let go. Then I would pray for her as follows:

You are relaxed and at ease, poised, serene, and calm. By day and by night you are prospering spiritually, mentally, and financially. You are a tremendous success. You are open and receptive to new ideas. Your good is flowing to you freely, joyously, endlessly, and ceaselessly. The law of increase is working for you now.

She would then pray for about five minutes in the same manner, affirming these truths in the first person and present tense. These weekly get-togethers brought marvelous results. Within a few weeks she began to make new contacts, and her sales increased by leaps and bounds. She discovered that a changed attitude changed everything in her life.

HIS SUBCONSCIOUS MADE HIM A MILLIONAIRE

Would you like me to show you how you can definitely and positively convey an idea or mental image to your subconscious mind?

Your conscious mind is personal and selective. It chooses, selects, weighs, analyzes, dissects, and investigates. It is capable of inductive and deductive reasoning. The subjective or subconscious mind is subject to the conscious mind. It might be called a servant of the conscious mind. The subconscious obeys the order of the conscious mind. Focused, directed thoughts reach the subjective level. They must be of a certain degree of intensity; intensity is acquired by concentration.

Ray M. worked his way through college by selling submarine sandwiches from dorm to dorm in the late evenings. He knew even then what he wanted: a chain of restaurants that would benefit him, his managers and employees, and the communities where they were located. He took courses in both business management and nutrition. By the time he graduated, he had enough savings to start his first restaurant. It was while this initial effort was still struggling that he came across a copy of my book *The Power of Your Subconscious Mind* (Paramus, NJ: Reward Books, 2000). It spoke to his ambitions, and it also offered practical ways to help bring those ambitions to fruition.

Ray followed the technique of impregnating his subconscious mind by concentrating on a successful initial public offering. To concentrate is to come back to the center and to contemplate the infinite riches of the subconscious mind. Every night, he stilled the activity of his mind and entered into a quiet, relaxed mental state. He gathered all his thoughts together and focused all his attention on seeing the stock of his restaurant corporation listed on the financial page of the newspaper. He gave all his attention to this mental image. His steadied attention made a deep, lasting impression on the sensitive plate of his subconscious mind.

He repeated this drama every night. A few weeks later, one of the diners in his restaurant came up to him after her meal. She was a former fellow student who remembered buying sandwiches from him on nights when she was studying late. Now she was a rapidly rising stock analyst with the most important brokerage firm in town. As they talked, it became clear that she not only liked the cuisine and the concept of Ray's restaurant, she also admired his ambition, zeal, enthusiasm, and dreams for accomplishment.

One thing led to another. Within the year, the two were married. Ray raised money from two venture capital firms to expand to several nearby communities. Incorporation and an IPO followed soon afterward, and Ray had the pleasure of picking up the morning paper and seeing his firm listed on the financial page.

PRAYER FOR PROSPERITY

Thou shalt make thy way prosperous, and then thou shalt have good success (Josh. 1:8). I now give a pattern of success and prosperity to the deeper mind within me, which is the law. I now identify myself with the Infinite Source of supply. I listen to the still, small voice of God within me. This inner voice leads, guides, and governs all my activities. I am one with the abundance of God. I know and believe that there are new and better ways of conducting my business; Infinite Intelligence reveals the new ways to me.

I am growing in wisdom and understanding. My business is God's business. I am divinely prospered in all ways. Divine Wisdom within me reveals the ways and means by which all my affairs are adjusted in the right way immediately.

The words of faith and conviction that I now speak open up all the necessary doors or avenues for my success and prosperity. I know that *the Lord* (Law) *will perfect that which concerneth me* (Ps. 138:8). My feet are kept in the perfect path, because I am a child of the living God.

SOME PROFITABLE POINTERS

1. Learn to use the laws of your mind, and you can attract to yourself wealth, love, happiness, and the life more abundant.

2. Decide to make money for others, and you will also make it for yourself; you will prosper beyond your fondest dreams.

3. Your subconscious mind has ways you know not of. Give it the idea of prosperity, and it will do the rest.

4. A wonderful prosperity formula is to affirm frequently and feelingly: "God multiplies my good exceedingly." Wonders happen as you pray in this way.

5. The thankful heart is always close to God. Use the Bible prayer: *Father, I thank thee that thou hast heard me. And I knew that thou hearest me always* (John 11:41–42). Lull yourself to sleep with "Thank you" on your lips.

6. You can decree a thing, and it shall come to pass, such as: "My home is free from all debt, and wealth flows to me in avalanches of abundance." Be sincere and mean it, and your subconscious will respond.

7. Life is addition. Add to your wealth, power, wisdom, knowledge, and faith by studying the law of your conscious and subconscious minds.

8. Affirm, "My good is flowing to me now, ceaselessly, tirelessly, joyously, and copiously," and God's riches will flow into your receptive, open mind.

9. You can convey the idea of wealth and success to your subconscious mind through concentration and focused attention. In due season, your subconscious will answer you in its own way. Two prerequisites are sincerity and undivided attention.

10. *Thou shalt make thy way prosperous, and then thou shalt have good success (Josh. 1:8).*

Law 14

The Penultimate Law of Creation

Napoleon said, "Imagination rules the world." Henry Ward Beecher said, "The mind without imagination is what an observatory would be without a telescope." Pascal wrote, "Imagination disposes of everything; it creates beauty, justice, happiness, which are everything in this world."

The faculty of image-making is called imagination. It is one of the primal faculties of mind. It has the power to project and clothe your ideas, giving them visibility on the screen of space. You can discipline, control, and direct your imagination constructively and get what you want in life, or you can use it negatively and imagine what you don't want in life. The mental images that you contemplate and consciously accept as true are impressed on your subconscious mind and made manifest in your life.

Imagination is the mighty instrument used by famous scientists, artists, poets, physicists, inventors, architects, and mystics. When the world says, "It is impossible, it can't be done," the person with a vivid imagination says, "It *is* done!"

HOW HE BECAME PRESIDENT

Fred Reinecke of Glendale, California became president of a major corporation as the result of the success power of his imagination. The following is from a letter he wrote to me, which he has given me permission to publish:

> I went into business with my brothers and sisters. Three months later, our business burned to the ground. We refused to go into bankruptcy or cry over spilt milk. We decided to rebuild, and I kept picturing in my mind a large corporation with salespeople all over the country.
>
> I pictured in my mind a great building, factory, offices, good facilities, knowing that through the alchemy of mind I could weave the fabric out of which my dreams would be clothed. You were of tremendous help to me, and you gave me a great lift on the occasion of my first visit to you, when you called me "Mr. President." You began to introduce me to others at church as "president of a multimillion-dollar corporation." Mentally, I had not quite accepted the title of president; it seemed an utter impossibility, as my brother was president.
>
> I began to think it over, and after a few weeks I accepted the title, "president," and affirmed, "I am president of my corporation in divine order. Either this or something grander or greater in the sight of Infinite Intelligence." I pictured a sumptuous office with my name on the door and the title, President's Office. I accepted it completely with a smile. It looked good to me!

Then things began to happen. First, a brother who was vice president decided to leave. Several months later, my other brother, the president of the corporation, announced that he was leaving to go into politics. My sister also left and attained a higher position in life. All members of my family are happy in their new undertakings, and I constantly pray for their guidance and true place in the same way as I pray for myself.

Now, suddenly, I was president! This enormous step that had seemed an impossibility only eighteen months before had become a reality, and today the business is flourishing beyond my fondest dreams. I believe implicitly what you teach—that "Imagination is the workshop of God."

HER CREATIVE IMAGINATION HEALED HER

Dr. Olive Gaze of Brentwood, California has tremendous faith and believes and understands the magical power of creative imagination. She is a lineal descendant of the world-famous preacher, Henry Ward Beecher. Dr. Gaze sent me the following letter on the power of constructive imagination:

Dear Dr. Murphy:

I was driving my late husband, Dr. Harry Gaze, and as we turned onto Sunset Boulevard, a frightful crash suddenly spun our car around; we both were rendered unconscious. When I came to, policemen were standing around us, and Harry was carried off in an ambulance. In my dazed state, I gave the policeman my doctor's home address and telephone number and your address and telephone number, which I never had memorized in my conscious mind. It was my subconscious speaking and acting. A most amazing thing is that I gave the policeman the name and exact address and telephone number of my maid, who was spending the weekend with her daughter in Woodland Hills; consciously, I did not know their address and had no idea of the phone number. This indicates true clairvoyance and is a perfect example of how the subconscious takes over.

I found myself in the hospital. My pelvis had been broken in several places, and I heard that I would not walk again. I began to imagine myself walking in to your lectures, and I pictured you shaking hands with me and congratulating me, saying, "You look wonderful! It is the miracle-working power of God."

I had absolute faith in the healing power of God, and while I was in the hospital I constantly pictured myself as doing all the things I ordinarily would do were I to be made whole. I kept affirming constantly: "God is healing me now. God made all the bones of my body, and they are all in their true place, ministering to me."

What I felt and imagined to be true came to pass. I now know that the creative power of God flows through our mental images. It is wonderful!

HER IMAGINATION HEALED HERSELF AND HER FAMILY

The following letter from Mrs. Fred Reinecke of Glendale, California is published with her permission:

Dear Dr. Murphy:

In a deep state of depression, I found myself locked up in the Camarillo State Mental Hospital. During clinical therapy, I met myself face to face; I learned to know myself and how to adjust to myself and others. I constantly affirmed, "God's love fills my soul, and He guides me." I got over the acute depression and was released.

I feel that God guided me to hear you lecture on the power of our subconscious minds. You stressed the amazing and miraculous power of mental imagery.

I began mentally to picture myself as happy, joyous, free, and prosperous. I mentally pictured a beautiful home, and many times a day I would sit down and picture my husband as a tremendous success, prosperous, and divinely happy. I would imagine that he was telling me how happy he was, how much he loved me, and how successful his business was. I pictured my daughter and son as they ought to be: brilliant students, industrious, and full of zeal and enthusiasm.

I steadily built the mental picture of a peaceful, happy, and joyous life; I lived with it daily. Per your instructions, every night I imagined that you were congratulating me on my inner peace, tranquillity, happiness, and freedom. I could see you smile, and I heard the tonal quality of your voice. I made it real and vivid, and all that I have mentally pictured for myself, my husband, and my two children has come to pass.

IMAGINING PRODUCES A GREAT TEACHER

While visiting the Round Towers of Ireland, I met a teacher named Patrick O. He seemed to be in a very pensive mood. I asked him, "On what are you meditating?"

"It is only by dwelling on the great and wonderful ideas of the world that we grow and expand," he replied. "I contemplate the age of the stones in the Towers. Then my

imagination takes me back to the quarries where the stones
were first cut and shaped. My imagination 'unclothes' the
stones. I see with my inner eye the structure, geological
formation, and composition of the stones reduced to the
formless state. Finally, I imagine the oneness of the stones
with all stones and all life. It is possible to reconstruct the
entire history of the Irish race from looking at the Round
Towers."

Through his imaginative faculty, Patrick was able to
see imaginary, invisible people living in the Towers and to
hear their voices. The entire place became alive to him in
his imagination. Through this power, he was able to go
back in time to when there were no Round Towers. In his
mind, he began to weave a drama of the place from which
the stones originated, who brought them, the purpose of the
structure, and the history connected with it. He said to me,
"I am able almost to feel the touch and hear the sound of
steps that vanished thousands of years ago."

As you can easily understand, Patrick is immensely
popular as a teacher and writer, and is widely sought after
as a lecturer. All of this is due to his practice of the faculty of imagination.

SCIENCE AND IMAGINATION

From the realm of imagination have come television, computers, radar, supersonic jets, and all other modern inventions. Your imagination is the treasure-house of infinity. It

releases from your subconscious mind all the precious jew-
els of music, art, poetry, and invention. You can look at an
ancient ruin, an old temple, or an Egyptian pyramid, and
you can reconstruct the records of the dead past. In the
ruins of an old churchyard, you also can see a modern city,
resurrected in all its former beauty and glory.

You may be in the prison of want and lack, or behind
stone bars, but in your imagination you can find an
undreamed-of measure of freedom.

GREAT ACCOMPLISHMENTS THROUGH IMAGINING

John Bunyan was in prison when he wrote his masterpiece
The Pilgrim's Progress. He used his imaginative faculty to
create such characters as Christian, Evangelist, Faithful,
Hopeful, and Giant Despair, who represent characteristics,
qualities, and patterns of behavior in all of us. These were
all fictitious characters, but as moods, feelings, beliefs,
attitudes, and capacities of human nature, they will live
forever in the hearts of people.

John Milton, though blind, saw with his inner eye. His
imagination brought forth *Paradise Lost*. In this way, he
brought some of God's Paradise to all people everywhere.
Imagination was Milton's spiritual eye; imagination
enabled him to go about God's business, whereby he anni-
hilated time, space, and matter and brought forth the truths
of the Invisible Presence.

IMAGINING BROUGHT HER SUCCESS AND RECOGNITION

Krista R., who had recently graduated from the University of California at Los Angeles, became a fixture at our meetings and lectures. One day when we were chatting, she said to me, "I feel certain I am called to be a writer, but the stories I send out always come back with a rejection form. I am beginning to be very discouraged."

"Don't be," I advised her. "Have you tried to create a story that would teach something about the Golden Rule? If you pass such a story and all of its characters through your spiritual and highly artistic mentality, I know you will create something that will be intensely interesting and instructive to your readers." I went on to suggest that, prior to sleep every night, she imagine that I was congratulating her on her success and on the acceptance of her story. Her visual imagery would sink into her subconscious mind and blossom there. If she persevered, results would follow.

Soon afterward, two magazines accepted stories of Krista's. She is now writing her first novel.

IMAGINING PROMOTED A CHEMIST

I was returning from a lecture tour in Europe when I got into a conversation with my seatmate, a young chemist named Jesse M. He told me about his first important success in his field, which was synthetic flavors and fragrances. For years his company had been working to synthesize a certain fragrance. Entire teams had tackled the problem, without success. The task was given up as hopeless. When Jesse came to work for the company, just out of graduate school, his superior gave him the job as a way of breaking him in. Jesse had no idea that his assignment was supposed to be impossible. A few weeks later, he presented his boss with a workable formula.

The others in the company were amazed. They wanted to know Jesse's secret. He told them that he had imagined the answer. That didn't satisfy them. He explained further: As he was preparing for sleep, he emblazoned the word "answer" in his mind, in blazing red letters. Under the word, he visualized a blank space in which the answer would appear. He followed this technique two nights in a row, without result. On the third night, he had a dream in which the complete formula and the technique for making the compound were clearly presented.

HOW IMAGINATION MAKES THE PAST ALIVE

Archaeologists and paleontologists studying the tombs of ancient Egypt, through their imaginative perception, reconstruct ancient scenes. The dead past becomes alive and audible once more.

Looking at the ancient ruins and the hieroglyphics

thereon, the scientists' imagination enables them to clothe the ancient temples with roofs and to surround them with gardens, pools, and fountains. The fossil remains are clothed with eyes, sinews, and muscles, and they again walk and talk.

The past becomes the living present, and we find that in imagination there is no time or space. Through your imaginative faculty, you can be a companion of the most inspired writers of all time.

GRADUATES WITH HONORS THROUGH IMAGINING

Michelle G. was a junior in high school when she started coming to our lectures on Sunday mornings on the subconscious mind. After a few weeks, she asked to speak with me privately. She confided that, while she had her heart set on going to college, and particularly a very selective private college nearby, her mother had told her it was out of the question. Her father, a firefighter, had been killed in a building collapse when Michelle was a baby. Her mother, who worked at a real estate agency, was just barely scraping by. There was nothing to spare in the family budget for an expensive college.

"I'm honored that you wanted to share this with me," I said. "But I don't think you need my advice. Do you?"

"No, I guess not," she replied. "I just have to practice what I've been learning, right?"

"Right," I said, with a smile.

Michelle got to work. Several times a day, she mentally created a beautiful, scenic drama. She imagined herself on campus, in the library and labs, sitting on the grass talking to other students. She saw the president of the college giving her her diploma, while the other students, in academic robes, applauded. She heard her mother congratulating her; she felt her mother's embrace and her kiss. She made it all real, natural, dramatic, exciting, and wonderful. She said to herself, "There is a creative intelligence in my subconscious mind with the power to mold all these forms I am picturing in my mind and to endow them with life, motion, and reality."

Michelle gave her visualizations greater reality by asking the college for its catalogue and viewbook and studying them intently. One day, her eye was drawn to a paragraph in small print in the back of the catalogue. It described a scholarship that had been established for children of members of the armed forces and uniformed civil services who were killed in the line of duty. Michelle called up to make an appointment with a financial aid officer at the college, who told her that she certainly did meet the requirements. If she could win admission to the college, the scholarship would cover her tuition, room, board, and other expenses!

Michelle's grades, test scores, and wonderful recommendations from teachers more than qualified her for the college and the scholarship. Her subconscious mind had given her more than compound interest. When she brought her acceptance letter to show me, she said, "My good came to me, pressed down, shaken together, and running over!" Four years later, she graduated magna cum laude. This is an example of the miracle-working powers of your imagination.

A BOY HEALED HIS MOTHER THROUGH IMAGINING

Justin P. was fourteen when I met him. He told me that whenever he had a problem, he would imagine that Jesus was talking to him, giving him the answer to his problem and telling him what to do.

This boy's mother was chronically ill. Frequently Justin would become still and quiet and imagine that Jesus was saying to him, "Go thy way; your mother is made whole!" He made that drama of his mind so real, vivid, and intense that, due to his faith and belief, he convinced himself of the truth of what he subjectively heard. His mother was completely healed; yet she had been considered beyond medical help.

Justin had galvanized himself into the feeling of being one with his image, and according to his faith or conviction was it done unto him. As he changed his mental attitude about his mother and imagined her perfect health, the idea of perfect health was simultaneously resurrected in his subconscious mind. There is but one healing power, namely, your subconscious mind. Justin had operated the law unconsciously, and he had believed in his own mind that Jesus was actually talking to him; then according to his belief, his subconscious responded.

This is why Paracelsus wrote in the sixteenth century, "Whether the object of your belief be true or false, you will get the same results."

IMAGINATION, THE WORKSHOP OF GOD

Where there is no vision, the people perish (Prov. 29:18). My vision is that I desire to know more of God and the way He works. My vision is for perfect health, harmony, and peace. My vision is the inner faith that Infinite Spirit heals and guides me now in all my ways. I know and believe that the God-Power within me answers my prayer; this is a deep conviction within me. I know that imagination is the result of what I image in my mind. *Faith is,* as Paul says, *the substance out of which the image is formed* (Heb. 11:1).

I make it my daily practice to imagine for myself and for others only that which is noble, wonderful, and God-like. I imagine that I am now doing the thing I long to do; I imagine that I now possess the things I long to possess; I imagine that I am what I long to be. To make it real, I feel the reality of it, and I know that it is so. Thank you, Father.

USING YOUR IMAGINATION

1. The faculty of image-making is called imagination. Imagination clothes all ideas and projects them on the screen of space.

2. You can picture a beautiful home, a trip, or a marriage and, as you feel its reality, your mental image will be objectified.

3. Imagine yourself doing what you love to do and feel yourself in the act, and wonders will happen in your life.

4. Mentally picture yourself as whole and perfect, living in a beautiful home, with a loving husband or wife, and with a happy, joyous family. Persevere in this mental image, and miracles will happen in your life.

5. Through disciplined imagination, you can see with your inner eye the structure of ancient ruins and, in your vivid imagination, you can reconstruct them and make the dead past seem to be alive.

6. It is the realm of imagination from which came television, computers, radar, and all other modern inventions.

7. Writers use the imaginative faculty to create the great works that have immortalized writers such as Shakespeare, Bunyan, Milton, and others.

8. Imagine that your writings will be fascinating and intensely interesting to the public, and imagine that you are being congratulated on your success. This habitual imagery will sink into your subconscious mind and eventually come to pass.

9. Through the practice of imagining a beautiful poem, song, or play that you have written, often the poem, the song, or the theme of the play will appear complete and ready in your mind without the slightest effort.

10. Chemists can imagine that they have the answer to a complex problem by contemplating the answer. Often, the answer will come in a dream, which is subconscious imagery, and the formula appears.

11. Looking at ancient ruins and the hieroglyphics thereon, the scientists' imagination enables them to clothe ancient temples with roofs and to surround them with gardens, pools, and fountains.

12. You can mentally create a beautiful, scenic drama that you wish would come to pass. Make it vivid, real, natural, dramatic, and exciting. Your subconscious mind will accept what you imagine and feel, and will bring it to pass.

13. You can imagine that a loved one is telling you that he or she has had a miraculous healing. Rejoice in

it, and see your loved one as vital and strong. Picture your loved one smiling, hear the good news, and feel the embrace, and you will galvanize yourself into the feeling of being one with your image. Your prayer will be answered!

LAW 15

THE ULTIMATE LAW OF INFINITE LIFE

The Omnipresence of God means that God, or Infinite Life, is present everywhere, at every moment of time and point of space. To practice the Presence of God all day long is the key to harmony, health, peace, joy, and the fullness of life. The practice of the Presence is powerful beyond imagination. Do not overlook it because of its utter simplicity.

You must realize that all creation is the expression of God in infinite differentiation. You are an individualized expression of God or Life, and God is forever seeking to express through you at higher and higher levels. Consequently, you are here to glorify God and to enjoy Him forever.

Begin now to contemplate the greatest of all truths, the all-inclusive and all-encompassing truth that God is the only cause, power, and substance in the world and that everything you see, feel, and touch is a part of His self-expression.

HOW TO BEGIN

I am acquainted with many people who sit down for five or ten minutes every day and meditate on the fact that God is absolute bliss, peace, harmony, joy, and infinite intelligence; who is all-powerful and who radiates boundless wisdom and infinite love. They let their thoughts dwell on these truths. They look at these qualities and powers of God from all angles. Then they begin to be aware that every person they meet is an expression of God. In fact, everything they see is God made manifest. It is God dramatizing Himself for the joy of expressing Himself. As they do this, people find their whole world changing. They consistently experience better health; their outer conditions improve; and they are possessed of a new vitality and energy.

HE FOUND HIS SON
AFTER SEVEN YEARS

Lawrence B., who attends my lectures, told me about an amazing episode in his life. About seven years ago, following a bitter divorce, his former wife disappeared with their son, who was then fourteen. Lawrence did everything he could think of to track them down, but his ex-wife was determined not to be found. Her revenge for the injuries she felt was to rob Lawrence of his only child forever.

In the last few months, however, Lawrence had become deeply interested in the practice of the Presence of God. He made it a practice, several times a day, to affirm, "My son is in the Presence of God, and God reveals to me where he is. I know that God brings both of us together in divine order, and I give thanks."

Shortly thereafter, Lawrence introduced me to his son. The young man had simply rung Lawrence's doorbell one afternoon, after being missing for seven long years!

At about the time Lawrence had begun to pray for his son's return, the young man was starting his own search. His mother refused to tell him anything at all about his father, so he didn't even know what part of the country he might be in. With the help of the internet, he made a list of every man in the United States and Canada with his last name and the first names Lawrence, Laurence, or Larry, or simply L. Then he began the tedious process of elimination. He was less than halfway through the list and beginning to become discouraged when he found himself staring at Lawrence B. in Los Angeles. He said it was as if the name were written in letters of fire. Instead of making his usual phone calls, he caught the next plane to the West Coast and took a taxi to the listed address!

For this my son was dead, and is alive again; he was lost, and is found. And they began to be merry (Luke 15:24).

HER HOME WAS SAVED

A few years ago a terrible forest and brush fire, driven by hurricane-force Santa Ana winds, swept the hills outside Los Angeles. Amanda V. phoned me frantically.

"I can see the line of fire at the crest of the hill behind the house," she told me. "It's coming this way. What should I do?"

I told her to join with me over the phone in practicing the Presence of God. We prayed as follows:

> We now acknowledge the Presence of God where you and your home are. Your home is surrounded with an envelope of God's love. The whole armor of God surrounds you and your home. You are immersed in the Omnipresence of God. The Presence of God is the cause of peace, harmony, joy, faith, and confidence. The sacred circle of God's eternal love surrounds your home and enfolds it, and God's Overshadowing Presence watches over it. We are now releasing this prayer, knowing that God answers.

Two hours later Amanda phoned me to say that the fire had burned right down to her back fence, then stopped! It seemed miraculous. Later that day a firefighter came by and said, "The only thing that could have saved your house is God Almighty."

SHE ACKNOWLEDGED THE PRESENCE

Elise G. was a junior editor in a large publishing firm in New York. She wrote to me to say that two women in the office were viciously gossiping about her and trying to undermine her position. The stories they were spreading were both grossly slanderous and wholly untrue.

I wrote back and suggested that Elise acknowledge the Presence of God in the women. This meant recognizing a superior wisdom, divine love, superior power, and divine harmony in them, while also recognizing the same powers and qualities in herself. I enclosed this prayer:

> I see the Presence of God in these women [mentioning their names]. God thinks, speaks, and acts through each of them. They are loving, kind, and cooperative. Whenever I think of one of them or meet one of them, I silently affirm, "God's love speaks through you. God is working through you."

Affirming this prayer was the only action Elise took. Within the next month, both women left to take jobs at other publishing houses. Before they left, each of them asked Elsie to lunch and expressed appreciation of her and a regret that they had not become better acquainted. The practice of the Presence dissolved everything unlike itself in the minds and hearts of these two women.

HIS AUDIENCE LOVES HIM NOW

Monroe A. was a young minister in his first appointment. He came to me for advice. "I don't understand it," he said. "The people in my congregation are so cold and distant. And my sermons . . . it makes me heartsick. I can't tell you how much time I spend preparing every week's sermon, or how careful I am to make sure every one of them adheres totally to the tenets of our faith. But all I get is criticism. Not to my face, of course, but the comments get back to me. Somehow I'm just not getting through to these people.

I don't know if it's mostly my fault or theirs, but this will show you how dire the situation is: I've been there almost a year now, and not once has a member of the congregation invited me to dinner!"

"That *is* bad," I said. "I suggest the practice of the Presence. Before you go onto the platform, radiate to the congregation love, peace, and good will, and affirm boldly for ten minutes: 'All those who come here this morning are blessed, healed, and inspired. God thinks, speaks, and acts through me. God is healing these worshippers through me. All who hear the words of truth pronounced by me are instantaneously healed, exalted, and prospered in a wonderful way. I love my congregation—they are God's children, and God's glory shines through them.'"

After a few weeks had passed, a miraculous change took place. Monroe's parishioners began to compliment him and tell him how they were helped and inspired by his sermons and how their prayers were answered in a wonderful way.

Monroe had discovered that the cure for every difficulty and problem is to practice the Presence of God. This Presence is the divine reality of every person, lying dormant beneath the superimposition of our human false beliefs, opinions, superstitions, and malconditioning.

HOW BROTHER LAWRENCE PRACTICED THE PRESENCE

Brother Lawrence was a seventeenth-century monk, a saintly man and wholly devoted to God. Possessing great

humility and simplicity, he was in tune with the Infinite.
"To do the will of God," he said, "is my whole business."

Brother Lawrence practiced the Presence when washing the dishes or scrubbing the floor. His attitude was that
it was all God's work. His awareness of the Presence of
God was no less when he was employed in the kitchen than
when he was before the altar. For Brother Lawrence, the
way to God was through the heart and through love. His
superiors marveled at this man who, although he was edu-
cated only to the point of reading and writing, could
express himself with such beauty and profound wisdom. It
was the inner voice of God that prompted all his sayings.

This is how Brother Lawrence practiced the Presence: He
said in effect, "I have put myself in your Presence; it is your
business that I am about, and so everything will be all right."

Brother Lawrence said that the only sorrow he could
experience would be the loss of the sense of His Presence,
but he never feared that, being wholly aware of God's love
and absolute goodness.

In his early life, Brother Lawrence feared that he would
be damned. This torture of his mind persisted for four
years. Then he came to see that the whole cause of this
negativity was lack of faith in God. Having become aware
of that, he was freed. He thereupon entered into a life of
continual joy.

Whether he was cooking, baking, or washing pans in
the kitchen, Brother Lawrence schooled himself to pause,
if only for a moment, to think of God in the center of his
being, to be conscious of God's Presence, and to keep a

hidden meeting with Him. Due to his inner illumination when he enjoyed the raptures of the Spirit, Brother Lawrence emerged into a realm of profound peace.

SHE HEALED HER SON

I received a letter from a businesswoman in Chicago named Jessica R. She had read in my book *The Miracle of Mind Dynamics* (Englewood Cliffs, NJ: Prentice Hall 1982), the chapter entitled "How to Be Well and Stay Well All the Time." It struck an important chord for her. Her son Kevin, who was eight, had been ill for about a year with chronic asthma. He often had paroxysmal attacks that sent him to the emergency room.

One night, Jessica sat by the bedside of her son after he went to sleep and prayed out loud:

Kevin, you are God's son. I see the Presence of God in you now. This is the presence of harmony, health, peace, joy, vitality, and wholeness. God breathed into you the breath of life. The Spirit of God made you, and I know the breath of the Almighty gave you life. You inhale the peace of God, and you exhale the love of God. *Father, I thank thee that thou hast heard me. And I knew that thou hearest me always* (John 11:41–42).

Jessica prayed in this way for about an hour, reiterating these great truths and knowing that they would sink into the subconscious of her son. At a certain point, she felt by

a sense of inner peace that her prayer was answered, and
she had no desire to go on praying any longer.

When Kevin woke up in the morning, he said,
"Mommy, last night an angel came to me and said I don't
have to have asthma any more. Isn't that super?" In the
days and weeks that followed, it became clear that the aths-
ma really was gone. The child had completely recovered.
His mother's conviction of the Presence of God communicated itself to her son, and his subconscious dramatized the
conviction in the symbolic form of an angelic figure that
told him he was made whole. This is a wonderful example
of the power of the practice of the Presence of God.

HE WALKED AND TALKED

Dr. Elsie McCoy of Beverly Hills, California gave me permission to cite the following miraculous healing:

> Mr. A. sustained severe head, neck, and chest injuries when a
> four-hundred-pound table fell on him. He was unconscious
> for several days. I called a minister to pray with me, and for
> about an hour we affirmed together, "God is the life of this
> man. He is alive with the life of God. The Presence of God in
> him is the presence of peace, vitality, and wholeness."
>
> At the end of that hour, Mr. A. regained consciousness,
> but he was unable to speak or walk because he was para-
> lyzed. It seemed like a hopeless case. I applied everything
> that I know in the healing arts, but I knew in my heart that
> only God could heal this man. The minister and I prayed
> with him every day, affirming, "God walks and talks in you.

You are speaking through the power of God, and you walk freely and joyously. We hear you talking to us, and we see you walking across the room. God is healing you now."

At the end of three months, the miracle happened. Mr. A. began to speak clearly, and he walked without crutches; he is still walking. His own statement was that he had heard everything that we said and drank it in. Undoubtedly, our prayers entered his subconscious mind, which responded. This was the result of the practice of the power of God to heal.

HE COULD NOT BE RUINED

While writing this chapter, I was interrupted by a long-distance telephone call from an old friend. His voice was strident and angry as he said, "My enemies are out to ruin and undermine me and my business." I suggested that he practice the Presence of God as follows:

These two men [his so-called enemies] are reflecting more and more of God and His goodness every day. They have the same hopes, desires, and aspirations as I have. They desire peace, harmony, love, joy, and abundance, and so do I. They are honest, sincere, and full of integrity, and divine justice reigns supreme. I wish for them all of God's blessings. Our relationship is harmonious, peaceful, and full of divine understanding. They wish to do the right thing according to the Golden Rule, as I do. I salute the Divinity within them, and I give thanks for the harmonious solution.

I told my friend to use this prayer many times a day and to let the impressions and feelings of these thoughts sink into his deeper mind until he was possessed by their truth. Furthermore, I told him that as he continued to bless in this way, he would feel a great sense of inner release, like a cleansing of the soul. I let him know that he would feel at peace and be relaxed.

He practiced the above technique in a whole-souled, devoted manner, and he discovered that he actually secreted the healing power from the depths of himself that brought about a perfect, harmonious solution to the problems he had with the men in question. A magnificent change took place among them. He discovered the practice of the Presence to be the all-encompassing truth that sets all people free.

PRACTICE THE THREE STEPS

The First Step

Accept the fact that God is the only Presence and the only power. God is the very life and reality of you.

The Second Step

Realize, know, and claim that everything you are and everything you see, whether it is a tree, dog, or cat, is a part of God's expression. This is the greatest thing you can do; it is powerful beyond words.

The Third Step

Sit down quietly two or three times a day, and think along these lines: "God is all there is; He is all in all."

Begin to realize that God indwells you and everyone around you. Remind yourself frequently that God is working and thinking through you and through other people as well, and especially remind yourself of this truth when dealing with or doing business with people.

If you sing, speak, act, or play an instrument in public, affirm silently, "God is blessing, prospering, and inspiring the audience through me." This will make them love and appreciate you. This is the real practice of the Presence of God.

DWELLING WITH GOD

I live in a state of consciousness. It is the consciousness of inner peace, joy, harmony, and good will for all humanity. I know that my real country is not a geographical location; a country is a dwelling place. I dwell in the Secret Place of the Most High; I abide in the Shadow of the Almighty; I walk and talk with God all the days of my life. I know that there is only one Divine Family, and that is humanity. *Let God arise, let his enemies be scattered* (Ps. 68:1).

I know that my only enemies are fear, ignorance, superstition, compromise, and other false gods. I will not permit these enemies to dwell in my mind. I refuse to give negative thoughts a passport to my mind. I enthrone God and His love in my mind. I think, feel, and act from the standpoint of divine love. I mentally touch the divine power now, and it moves in my behalf; I feel invincible. Peace begins with me. I feel God's river of peace flowing through me now.

I claim that the love of God permeates the hearts of all humanity, and God and His wisdom rule, guide, and govern me and all people everywhere. God inspires me, our leaders, and the governments of all nations to do His will, and His will only. The will of God is harmony, peace, joy, wholeness, beauty, and perfection. It is wonderful!

RECALLING GREAT TRUTHS

1. The practice of the Presence is the key to health, happiness, and peace of mind.

2. Begin to realize that everything you see is some part of the self-expression of God.

3. God is Infinite Intelligence; if your child is lost, it knows where the child is and will reveal to you the child's whereabouts.

4. Nothing can touch you or your home if you surround yourself with a circle of God's love and know that his Overshadowing Presence protects you.

5. See the Presence of God in the other who is troublesome or who is gossiping about you. Claim that God thinks, speaks, and acts through that person, and you will discover that love never fails.

6. If you are a speaker or lecturer, affirm, "God is blessing and healing the audience through me," and wonders will happen in your life.

7. All work is God's work. Whatever work you are engaged in, do it for the glory of God.

8. You can pray for a member of your family by realizing the presence of God's love, peace, joy, and harmony. Feel the reality of what you affirm, and the subconscious of your loved one will respond accordingly.

9. If people are trying to hurt you, realize that you are one with God, and they cannot penetrate your defense. Bless them by realizing that they are honest, sincere, and loving, and that they are governed by God and by God alone. There will inevitably be a harmonious solution.

10. Realize that everything you see, regardless of what it is, is part of God's expression; this is the greatest thing you can do. Every person you meet is an incarnation of God. Every person is waiting for you to overlook his or her frailties, shortcomings, and derelictions. Like Paul of Tarsus, try to see the Christ in each person, the hope of glory.

INDEX

Actualization, 26–27. *See also* Imagery

Affirmations. *See also* Prayer
  daily, 14
  divine guidance, 87, 89, 117, 138, 190–91
  dreams, accomplishing, 42, 85, 96, 136, 140–41
  emotional control, 160, 163
  eyes and ears, 52–53
  faith, 19, 73–74, 117, 138, 231, 232
  fear, casting out, 146–47
  forgiving, 7, 56–57, 95, 188
  healing, 37, 40, 50, 114, 146, 235
  imagining, 224
  marital harmony, 171–72, 173, 180–81, 187
  mental attitude, improving, 99–100, 106–7, 126, 146, 171–72
  peace of mind, 23, 86, 106–7, 112, 117, 128–29, 136, 140–41, 186, 188, 190–91,
  Presence of God, practicing, 231, 232, 235, 237, 239–40
  prosperity, 207, 209
  security, 112, 114, 117, 119, 126, 128–29, 130
  spirit-voices, overcoming, 34–35
  transforming life, 72–74
  worry, overcoming, 196–97

Agoraphobia, 129–30
Anxiety neurosis, 187–89
Attitude
  changing, 101, 108
  improving, 99–100, 106–7, 126, 146, 171–72

Bible, words from, 1, 2, 3, 7, 14, 16, 17, 20, 25, 28, 29, 37, 39, 42, 45, 47, 52, 54, 64, 97, 114, 118, 120, 122, 126, 127, 128, 147, 162, 163, 175, 180, 183, 192, 203, 206, 209, 211, 224, 230, 235
Blaming others, 104, 145. *See also* Hatred; Resentment
Blind faith, definition of, 44
Body, effect of emotions on, 72–74, 76, 156–57, 187, 193–94
Bunyan, John, 218
Businesspeople, guidance for, 21–24, 65–66, 79–81, 140–41, 189–91. *See also* Prosperity

Cancer, miraculous healing of, 56–58
Cause and effect, 105, 108
Children
  response to healing, 36–37. 235–36
  worrying about, 60–61, 192, 198
Choose, capacity to, 97–98, 102–3, 107, 108
Clairaudience, 34

Combat, prayers during, 93–94,
    156
Confined, being, 93–94, 107
Courage, law of, 90–108
Coveting another person's spouse,
    174–77, 182
Creation, law of, 212–27. *See also*
    Imagery

Daily prayer, 14
Decision making, 28–29, 80–81,
    95–97, 107
Depression, 151–53, 215–16
Diet, importance of, 124–27, 131
Divine guidance, prayer for, 87, 89
Divorce, 169–72, 178–79
Double-mindedness, overcoming,
    101–2, 108
Dropsy, miraculous healing of,
    48–50

Ears, prayer for, 52–33
Emotional control, law of, 149–65
Envy, 51, 124
Eyes, prayer for, 52–53

Failure, fear of, 92–93, 107
Faith
    blind vs. true, 44–45
    degrees of, 38
    invisible power of, 20–21, 27–28,
        30
    secret law of, 17–31
Fear, 67, 94–95, 99, 101, 107, 108,
    142–45
Fear thoughts, 142, 148
Financial disaster, prayer and, 12–14
Fleeting impression, 83

Forgiveness, 6–7, 56–57, 74, 95, 107
Frustration, 98–100, 107–8

Gaze, Olive, 214–15
God. *See also* Infinite Intelligence
    belief about, 57–58, 63–66
    dwelling with, prayer for, 239–40
    law of Infinite life, 228–41
    love of, 136
    power of, 1–16, 73–74
    Presence of, 228–41
    response of, 27–28, 31
    spiritual treatment and, 45

Hand, as symbol, 41–42
Hatred, 51, 55–57, 72–73, 74, 99, 124,
    134, 153
Healing
    of dropsy, 48–50
    faith and 42–45
    miraculous healing, 32–54,
        223–24, 226–27, 235–37
    mood changes for, 36–37
    of palsy, 38–40
    spirit-voices, 33–35
    steps in, 50–51, 53–54
    universal principle, 48
Heaven
    creating your own, 104–5, 108
    definition of, 5

Imagery, 26–27, 61, 93–94, 129–30,
    200, 202, 204
Imagination, 212–27. *See also*
    Imagery
    healing through, 223–24
    science and, 217–18
Increase, law of, 203–4, 207

Incurable, facing the word, 47–48
Infinite Intelligence, 1, 2, 5, 8, 9, 10,
    28–29
    faith in, 28–29
Infinite life, law of, 228–41
Inner guidance
    being receptive to, 83–84, 88
    law of, 77–89
Intuition, 84–85
Investments, 115–16, 121

Jealousy, 67, 104, 124, 134, 138–39

Lawrence, Brother, 223–25
Loneliness, 58–60, 170
Loss, sense of, 67, 117–20
Love
    of God, 136
    law of, 133–48
    transforming power of, 69–71

Marital harmony, law of, 166–83
    biblical formula, 180
Maturity, 150, 163
McCoy, Elsie, 236–37
Mental nutrition, law of, 123–32
Mental vision, 93–94, 107
Milton, John, 138, 218
Mind. *See also* Subconscious mind
Miracle
    as confirmation of all possibilities,
        47
    of prayer, 2–4
    of three steps, 66–68

Miracle of Mind Dynamics, The, 235
Miraculous healing, 32–54, 223–24,
    226–27, 235–37

of cancer, 56–58
of dropsy, 48–50
imagination and, 223–24, 226–27
of palsy, 38–40
Natural-born healer, 37–38
Ninety-first Psalm, 62, 74

Palsy, miraculous healing of, 38–40
Panic, being freed from, 90–92
Paradise Lost, 218
Peace of mind, law of, 184–98
Personal inventory, taking, 102–3, 108
Pilgrim's Progress, The, 218
Power of Your Subconscious Mind,
        The, 208
Prayer
    changing your life through, 4,
        15–16
    daily, 14
    examples. See Affirmations
    power of, 1–4, 15–16
    three steps of, 50–51, 66–68,
        196–97, 238–39
Presence of God, 228–41
Prisoner, prayer and, 10–12
Prosperity, automatic, law of, 199–211
Protection, law of, 55–76
Psalms, words of, 1, 37, 54, 62, 74,
        128, 158, 192, 195, 199
    Ninety-first, 62, 74
    Twenty-third, 37
Psychosomatics, 157
Punishment, fear of, 94–95, 107

Quimby, Phineas Parkhurst, 49, 75

Racial prejudice, overcoming, 9–10
Reform, desire to, 3

Reinecke, Fred, 213–14
Reinecke, Mrs. Fred, 215–16
Relaxed, being, 83–84, 88
Repression of emotion, 157
Resentment, 51, 99, 104, 134
Retribution and reward, 105–6, 108
Reuniting, 68–69
Romantic life, 58–59. *See also* Marital
    harmony

Science and imagination, 217–18
Security, law of, 109–22
Self-image, 150–51, 179
Selye, Hans, 193–94
Shyness, 58–60
Spiritual blindness, 51–52, 54
Spiritual treatment, 45–47
Spirit-voices, 33–35
Steps, three. See Three steps in
    prayer
Subconscious mind
    blocking, 95–98, 107
    conscious vs. subconscious, 51–52,
      207–9
    Infinite Intelligence in, 77, 87, 88
    influencing, 104–5, 207–9
    law for Lord, 139–40

Sublimation, 152–53
Substitution, law of, 157–58
Temper, overcoming, 153–54
Thank you, saying, 204–5
Thoughts
    fear, 142, 148
    wise, 97, 107
Three steps in prayer
    for healing, 50–51
    miracle of, 66–68
    for overcoming worry, 196–97
    for practicing Presence of God,
      238–39
Transformation of self, 161–62
True faith, definition of, 44
Twenty-third Psalm, 37

Ups and downs of life, 116–17, 122

Vision, spiritual, 52, 54
Visualization. See Imagery

Wise thoughts, 97, 107
Withered hand, as symbol, 40–42
Worry, overcoming, 195–97. *See also*
    Peace of mind
Writer, prayer for, 85, 89–90